Images of History

Nineteenth and Early Twentieth Century Latin American Photographs as Documents

Robert M. Levine

DUKE UNIVERSITY PRESS • DURHAM AND LONDON • 1989

For Peggy and Joey

© 1989 Duke University Press

All rights reserved

Printed in the United States of America on acid-free paper ∞

Library of Congress Cataloging-in-Publication Data

Levine, Robert M.

Images of history : nineteenth and early twentieth century

Latin American photographs as documents / by Robert

M. Levine.

Bibliography: p.   Includes index.

ISBN 0-8223-0883-5.

1. Latin America—History—1830-1898—Pictorial works.

2. Latin America—History—1830-1898. 3. Latin America

—History—1898-1948—Pictorial works. 4. Latin Amer-

ica—History—1898-1948. 5. Latin America—Descrip-

tion and travel—Views. 6. Photography—Latin America

—History. 7. Photography in historiography. I. Title.

F1413.L66   1989

980'.03—dc19   88-26741 CIP

Contents

Acknowledgments

WHILE putting together the materials from which this book was written, many persons offered kinds of assistance without which the work would never have been completed. I am grateful to H. L. (Hack) Hoffenberg for putting his fine collection in New York at my disposal and for introducing me to Gilberto Ferrez and Elyn Welsh, as well as Joana and Didí dos Santos in Salvador. Hack not only invited me to speak at the opening of his second (and best) show at the Center for Inter-American Relations in New York City, but he provided direct assistance for the production of the videotaped documentary "Imagenes de Reinos," which was ultimately produced in English, Spanish, Portuguese, and Chinese, and which won the 1986 Award of Merit of the Latin American Studies Association. "Imagenes de Reinos" explored the ways in which nineteenth-century photographers interpreted Latin America, and utilized many of the photographs published in this volume.

I would like to acknowledge the staffs of the following libraries, photographic archives, and research centers, and other individuals in Latin America: the Chambi family in Cuzco; the Rodriguez family in Morococha; the Biblioteca Nacional in Caracas; the Biblioteca Nacional in Rio de Janeiro; the Fundação Casa Rui Barbosa, also in Rio de Janeiro (and Eduardo Silva, a historian at the Casa interested in photographs as documents); the Museu do Imagem e do Som in São Paulo (and Boris Kossoy, its former Director); Carlos Forman; the Museu Rodrigues Alves and Museu Histórico Frei Galvão in Guaratinguetá, in São Paulo State; the Arquivo Público in Salvador (and its director, Consuelo Pondé de Sena); the Instituto Geográfico e Histórico, also in Salvador (and its director, Thales de Azevedo); Renato Ferraz and Iara Bandeira de Ataíde of the Centro de Estudos Euclydes da Cunha; Antônio Marcelino in Salvador; the Fundação Joaquim Nabuco in Recife; Marc Hoffnagel of the Universidade Federal de Pernambuco; Carlos Bakota; Cesar Naus of UNEB in Salvador; Mário Cravo Neto and Mário Cravo Filho; in São Paulo, José Carlos Sebe Bom Meihy and Federico Nasser; Eduardo Serrano in Bogotá; and Lic. Bernardo Vega in Santo Domingo.

In the United States and Canada, I wish to acknowledge the help of the staff of the Library of Congress (Madison Building); the Tulane University Latin American Library (Thomas Niehaus, Director); David Howell and Barbara Brocato in New Orleans; The State Historical Society of Wisconsin in Madison; Edward Ranney in Santa Fe, who put me in touch with the Chambi family in Cuzco; and Stella de Sá Rêgo at the University of New Mexico in Albuquerque. Ramiro Fernandez, who owns one of the finest collections of nineteenth-century photographs of Cuba, kindly permitted me to reprint some of his images. In Coral Gables, Carlos Monge and his wife Tití deserve thanks, as do Steve Stein, Nada Massey, Lenny del Granado, Alan Belitsky, Germán Mejía, Louise Strauss, Mark D. Szuchman, and David F. Graf. Nora Elena Vélez kindly put me in touch with Eduardo Serrano and brought me his book. I also wish to thank Craig Hendricks, Catherine Lugar, Yi-Fu Tuan, and Jackie Austin, and the staff of the California Museum of Photography in Riverside. Professional colleagues E. Bradford Burns, Warren Dean, José B. Fernandez, Geraldine Forbes, Sandra Lauderdale Graham, Gilbert M. Joseph, Catherine LeGrand, Kathleen Logan, Joseph L. Love, Jr., Frank D.

McCann, and William R. Taylor, among others, lent advice and encouragement.

Sidney Sorkin introduced me to photography as a youngster and I thank him. At the University of Miami Word Processing Center, special thanks go to Ana Miyares.

Few of the more than two hundred photographs reproduced in this volume have ever been examined as historical documents, and many have never been published at all. Permission to reproduce the photographs was given by the individuals and institutions listed in the section "Sources of the Photographs." I am very appreciative of their cooperation. It is my hope to demonstrate the range and significance of historical photographs of Latin America through the selections I have made. I will be grateful if this book complements other materials used to learn about the Latin American past.

Robert M. Levine
Coral Gables
March 1988

Introduction

A good half of what one sees is seen through the eyes of others.—Marc Bloch, The Historian's Craft

PHOTOGRAPHS provide a rich and special source of documentation of the past. They illustrate historical narrative as well as offer evidence on which to frame new hypotheses or with which to test old ones. Photographic images are slowly being "discovered" by social historians, thus it has become necessary to debate criteria for interpretation. But fearing that analysis of historical photographs must, by definition, be fatally subjective, scholars have tended to tiptoe lightly over photographic content. As a result, most authors who include photographs in their published writings employ them to illustrate, not to explain.

A few scholars have employed visual evidence in imaginative ways. Gilberto Freyre culled nineteenth-century Brazilian newspaper announcements of runaway slaves to find descriptive evidence of heavy work or mistreatment: scars inflicted by punishment, bald spots caused by the friction of heavy weight carried on slaves' heads, horny callouses on fingers and knees from stoop labor.[1] Over the years a few

publishers have acknowledged historical photographs. Anita Brenner's *The Wind that Swept Mexico* (1943) used 184 images selected by George R. Leighton to illustrate her sympathetic narrative of the Mexican Revolution. Agustín Víctor Casasola's son prepared an expanded edition of the photographer's 1921 *Album histórico gráfico*, a photographic record of prerevolutionary and revolutionary Mexico.[2] Paul Vanderwood and Frank Samponaro have published a new study of the Mexican Revolutionary Era (1910 to 1917) using postcard images.[3]

Social scientists use photographs in a variety of ways. Anthropologists look for patterns after careful scrutiny and measurement of detail. They inventory the contents of photographs, listing not only items (possessions in a home, for example) but also devising inventories of cultural significance, removing details wholly from the visual, counting and studying them. Anthropologists also study transformation photos, images showing indigenous peoples first in their native dress, then in "European" attire.[4] They measure proxemics (space), kinesics (body behavior), and choreometrics (patterns of behavior). This kind of visual anthropology rec-

ognizes that camera vision differs from the observing human eye, which is narrow of field and selective. Precisely because it is mechanical, the camera eye is the "least disturbed" visual record available.[5] Historians, on the other hand, do not have the luxury of being able to photograph the subjects they wish to analyze, nor do they usually have access to large quantities of older photographs.

This book examines how photography helped define the ways Latin Americans came to see themselves and the world. It focuses on the evolution of Latin American photography from its earliest origins in the late 1830s to the rise of mass communications and the accompanying saturation of the public with photographic images by the 1920s and 1930s.

Before this cultural watershed, when photographers began to venture beyond their studios onto city streets and into the countryside, most onlookers had never seen a camera. Unless they came from a higher social class than the photographer, subjects posed awkwardly, consciously looking into or away from the lens.[6] Photographs taken under such conditions reveal not only visual facts but, to some extent, attitudes, relationships, and perhaps even values.

Formal photographs by professionals and candid shots taken by amateurs hold equal value for this study. As the poor acquired the means to be photographed, even if only on special occasions, they created the basis for a visual history of people who otherwise would be unremembered.[7]

A photograph becomes a historical document when it suggests ways to examine people's lives or when it captures the texture of daily life.[8] Obviously, it is one thing to extract material evidence from a photograph, and very much another to attempt to extract emotional, psychological, or personal inferences from mute images for which we lack supplementary data. Things become a bit easier when the "facts" of a photograph are linked with others to form a pattern that is understandable and credible.[9] But since people see images in so many different ways, the kind of contextual evidence which photographs provide should be seen as provocative and suggestive rather than definitive. Photographs do permit us to glimpse at individual lives. This is what gave Agee and Evans's *Now Let Us Praise Famous Men* its power: the book did not abstractly deal with "people" or "masses"; it portrayed individual members of three sharecropper families.

Photographs probe beneath the surface of generalization to offer concrete evidence of social conditions. Since manipulation of photographic composition occurs to a greater extent when the photographer is highly skilled (or when the photographer simply spends time thinking about his or her desired final image), photographs taken by amateurs may be more useful than images produced by professionals. Even "artless" family albums reflect social styles and conventions.[10] Such images, after the passing of the heyday of studio portraitists, were considered vulgar and "drastically reduced in value."[11] But whatever the liabilities (through amateurism) or pretensions (through artistry) of the individual photographer, a photograph —any photograph—seems to have a relatively innocent, and therefore relatively accurate, relation to visible reality.[12] The difficulty comes not with what family photographs show, but with what they omit. Ever since the late nineteenth century, when photograph taking became relatively accessible, family photography has fallen into ritualistic exercise, memorializing ceremo-nial family occasions but overlooking the ordinary, even banal, aspects of everyday life. Family photographs in Latin America, as elsewhere, depict the full cycle of life events, including death (photographs of dead infants dressed as angels were common throughout the nineteenth century), but they generally do not show family discord or misfortune. Eugen Weber suggests that when we began to view photography as a way to fix events solemnly for eternity, the act of photographing became a formal ritual, robbed of spontaneity.[13]

Photographs of family life reveal relationships and hint at attitudes. We know that in the mid-nineteenth century elite children in Latin America, especially boys, were required to act like miniature adults. Were the doleful faces peering into the camera the same faces worn by boys throughout the entire day, or were they put on for the photographer? Does the fact that boys paraded down the street in stuffy formal clothing, usually wearing formal black hats, reflect only sartorial fashions or does it suggest deeper social inhibitions?[14]

Photographs provide tangible detail. They indicate religion, ethnicity, elements of order and disorder, economic status, tastes, attitudes, and human relations. Members of different socio-economic groups, for instance, respond to the camera according to their cultural patterns. Upper-class persons march through space, hurrying, seemingly purposeful; Indians seem to be drifting, or moving without purpose.[15] Lower-class individuals reveal different mannerisms depending on where the photograph is taken. Posing at their work, or alongside members of the elite, they may appear passive or lazy. Protected within their own society, they may be relaxed, behaving by their own rules, acting according to different hierarchies of status. If the photographer represents the authority or power of the elite, subjects will pose as society dictates.[16] Early photographers were feared and were seen as practitioners of mesmerism.[17] Only the most self-assured possessed the courage to sit taking the camera dead on.

In Latin America most photographers working in smaller cities and towns remained inside their studios where they could more easily give their subjects the attributed status and sobriety which they paid the photographer to provide.

Given that Latin American society tended to deny evidence of social inequality, photographers there perhaps took greater pains to mask distress and to produce appealing images.

Writing about urban diversity, novelist Italo Calvino proposed that "many seemingly different urban places are really the same."[18] Photographs can reveal multiple functions for locations, documenting changing patterns and activities. The ways that photographers selected and composed their scenes of daily life comprises another element of photographic analysis. Wanting to emphasize progress and order, they took pains to select camera angles, times of day, and lens-to-subject distances that contributed to such results. They relied on conventions and habits of pictorial representation consistent with their ability to manipulate the final appearance of their visual image.

This book is divided into two parts: an analysis of the evolution of Latin American photography in the context of Latin American history, and a "hands on" section, which discusses the use of photographs in historical analysis. The first two chapters, "The Daguerreotype Era" and "Order and Progress," examine the ways in

which photographers (not unlike writers, politicians, and even historians) borrowed from the ideologies and goals of the prevailing elite culture and helped shape the ways in which Latin Americans (and others) came to see their world. Photographers documented the region's thirst for material progress, social stability, and cultural achievement. Each chapter also contrasts Latin American trends with developments in North America and in Europe, when appropriate. Part two of the book (chapters 3 and 4) deals with content evaluation. "Reading Photographs" proposes guidelines for historical analysis; "Posed Worlds and Alternate Realities" is an annotated photo essay contrasting posed photographs with "accidental" or spontaneous photographs, uncontrived for purposes of legitimation or explanation.

Some of these photographs were taken by famous photographers, but most came from the lenses of cameramen about whom little is known or who were anonymous. This does not matter. In *Images of History* the photographic images, not their pedigree, are my principal concern.

Part One   Photography and Society

IN THE Luso-Hispanic portions of the New World the dynastic ties which bound the colonies to Madrid and Lisbon relied on a tightly knit social structure. Formal and closely monitored, the relationship aimed to recreate Spain and Portugal in America. Among the dominant classes this relationship not only fostered narrow dependence on the mother country but also led to a distaste for local culture, which was considered "uncivilized" by the new Latin American elites. Photography, emerging in the mid-nineteeth century in the aftermath of political independence, provided a powerful medium for the projection of a modern and progressive image of the region.

In Mexico and Peru, the leading centers of Spanish colonization, agents of the crown rooted out the architectural symbols of Indian life just as ruthlessly as they carried away the gold and silver that had adorned them. In Brazil, less central to the Portuguese Empire (which considered the Far East and Africa to be of greater importance until the discovery of large deposits of gold in the mountainous interior of Minas Gerais in the 1590s), the difficulty of enslaving Indians led to the importation of Africans to work the plantations and mines.

Throughout colonial Latin America, the elite—drawn from the greater and lesser ranges of Iberian nobility—felt compelled to exorcise "primitive," embarrassing elements from society. They were influenced by the enlightenment's view of science as the preeminent mode of truth. Politically, Spain and Portugal imposed on this class an elaborate bureaucracy empowered to keep the colonies on a tight leash. Officials operated according to an unspoken compact: colonial elites would preserve royal authority and keep the lower classes in check. In return, the crown would grant honors, benefits, and latitude in observing the law. Cultural creativity was stifled; artisanship remained minimal and industry was forbidden. Using peninsular brokers as required by the colonial mercantile system, wealthy families imported furniture, china, and art objects from Northern Europe and Italy. The result was a closed society, one which was in most ways isolated from the rapidly changing world of Western Europe.

Over time a dual Latin American elite evolved. A thin layer of peninsular-born appointees and their immediate families occupied the top levels of the hierarchy. These *peninsulares* reigned over a second layer composed of their New World-born offspring who chose to remain. This stratum—the Creoles —was equally well bred, but in the eyes of the colonial system, was socially inferior. Affluent and locally powerful as time passed, the Creoles began to chafe at their second-rank status.

Some dealt with the "rustic" label applied to them by *peninsulares* by trying to become more cultivated and more elegant than the newly arriving European officials. Indifferent to the brilliant environment in which they lived, they sealed themselves within the boundaries of their towns and cities. Their evolving self-image nurtured itself on their nation's outer borders and defined itself in terms of foreign reality.[1]

Creoles considered the interior of the continent to be untamed, topographically forbidding, and populated with savages—the subject of scientific curiosity for European travellers and naturalists, but not a basis for national pride. Rather than celebrate the native environment, Latin American elites disparaged it. When intellectuals finally acknowledged the presence of indigenous populations, nearly two generations after political independence, they did so romantically. The indigenous culture was described in airy, spiritual terms, essentially not changing the elite's distaste for the Indian, African, and mestizo cultures which stubbornly survived in their midst.[2]

Liberalization of the mercantile system as part of the late eighteenth-century colonial reforms brought increased prosperity, especially to formerly peripheral colonies such as La Plata in the south and Gran Colombia in northern South America. Improved conditions only fed the Creole elite's frustration. Some Creoles were influenced by the rebellion of the British North American colonies, others by the ideas (but not the outcome) of the French Revolution after 1789. Spain's New World empire was thrown to its own devices by the Napoleonic invasion of the Iberian peninsula in 1808, and fragmented into more than a dozen independent republics by 1824. Brazil followed suit only partially, proclaiming its independence in 1822 but retaining both the monarchy and the Bragança dynasty. Throughout the region the old cultural dependence on Spain and Portugal yielded to new forms of neo-colonial dependence. More than

ever elites aligned their tastes to French, English, Italian, and North American fashion.

Despite the apparent changes in the political formulations of post-colonial society, the nineteenth-century Latin American economy remained primarily rural and agricultural. The estates and plantations as well as the mines continued to be worked by Indian, mestizo, and mulatto laborers (and until the late 1880s in Brazil and Cuba, by black slaves). City growth was based on commerce, not industry, since manufactured goods were imported by middlemen in exchange for raw material exports. Foreigners, not the locally-born, dominated overseas trade in every Latin American country except Colombia. For this reason, many of the foreign merchants amassed wealth and power, but not status, which remained in the control of the Creole elite descended from the colonial aristocracy.[3]

In the early part of the nineteenth century conditions were harsh. Trade virtually ceased between 1810 and 1826; adjacent states quarreled. Internal regionalist revolts sapped the energies of central governments, fragmented efforts to achieve national integration, and facil-

itated the dictatorships of strong-armed *caudillos* ("leaders") like Rosas in Argentina and Santa Ana in Mexico. Pressing debt and the desire to build railroads, bridges, port facilities, and roads accelerated borrowing from foreign lenders, creating a new matrix of neo-colonial dependency which later would have pernicious effects. Latin America exported primary products—coffee, tin, nitrates, sugar, cotton, hides, dried beef, copper, guano—and imported every kind of manufactured product, from railroad engines to hat pins.

Invariably, European firms were awarded public works contracts. As a result, every Latin American city of any size sported a burgeoning colony of foreign managers, bankers, engineers, architects, technicians, and their families. Although these foreigners did not mix socially (they were not encouraged to do so, nor did they try to), the elites deferred to them because they were seen as holding the key to making the urban New World like Paris and London.

Owners of plantations and the massive holdings in the interior maintained near total dominance over rural life. The emerging urban upper class—the brokers, importers, factors—

prospered (as did the foreign merchants and bankers) as long as prices for raw goods remained high on the world market. Military (and later political) service provided mestizos with some opportunities for social mobility, but the traditional families remained dominant, increasing their power by expanding their holdings and ignoring politics, which was characterized by instability since it did not fit into the neo-colonial free-trade pattern. Although the North Atlantic economy expanded rapidly in the nineteenth century, Latin America stood on its periphery, and its elites were content to react passively by accepting foreign stewardship in fiscal matters, trade, and high-cost imported technology.[4]

Artists and naturalists arrived in Latin America to join the many scientific expeditions sponsored by European societies and governments. Painters and illustrators came to record the discoveries and to bring back sketches and paintings of the wilderness. These artists, *costumbristas*, were skilled in reproducing at a rapid pace the most exhaustive detail with pen and ink. Their presence highlighted the growing difference between the foreign view of Latin

America—a place of natural wonder, romantically exotic—and the Creole elite's desire to tame the wilderness and suppress the exotic landscape.

Other craftsmen came independently, drawn by the lure of the unknown and what they considered to be opportunities to make a living. Few of the specialists attracted to Latin America came from Spain and Portugal; lacking the French, English, and German tradition of secular academies dedicated to experimental science, the Spanish and Portuguese grudgingly permitted others to enter their territories for scientific purposes, but not until the end of the eighteenth century. Local interest picked up during the period of Bourbon reform, especially after 1759, but the scientists and naturalists continued to be Europeans. The situation in Brazil was the same. The Dutch promoted a flurry of agricultural and engineering experiments during their occupation of Pernambuco after 1630, but a decade later, after Portugal restored its territorial control, scientific efforts became restricted to finding commercial uses for native plants and animals.[5]

In the aftermath of political independence,

the peninsular cultural legacy was cast aside entirely, except for that which remained in the religious practices of the small upper class. Even in the waning years of colonial rule, the cultural axis had shifted from Spain to France. Technology was considered an Anglo-Saxon product and was much sought after. Some cities in the Southern Hemisphere acquired street lighting, for example, well before their North American counterparts. Many Latin American cities boasted theaters, opera houses, parks, and zoological gardens, and by the second part of the century many had up-to-date water supply systems.

In the fine arts French culture reigned supreme. One of the direct consequences of this open channel of cultural contact was that photography, which developed simultaneously in various parts of the world in the 1830s but whose initial development took place in France, was enthusiastically embraced in the New World. Photography enthralled Latin Americans for many reasons. It epitomized modernity; it combined the aesthetic of art with the precise world of science; and it was wildly fashionable in Europe. The most immediately far-reaching and popular of all nineteenth-century inventions, photography stunned viewers, "upsetting all previous ideas of what was even possible."[6]

In this early period, before it became a mass art form and a social rite, photography served elites as a tool of power.[7] Photographers could not only document the exotic nature of the New World, but their work could be done methodically, under controlled conditions. The elite's sense of social distance could be preserved; the untamed aspect of the land and its peoples could be softened. Photographic tools could be employed to combat the distorted popular image of the New World among educated Europeans—an image spawned by the romance of discovery and conquest, noble and ignoble savages, and the legends of El Dorado, Gran Quivira, the Seven Cities of Cibola, and the Nation of the Amazons—all of which were distasteful to upper-class Latin Americans who wished to be considered urbane and civilized.

Photographic beginnings

Since their introduction camera-produced images were believed to represent reality. In fact, the fifteenth-century discovery of linear perspective, which immensely improved attempts at rendering accurate images through art, contributed to photography's origins.[8] Photographers, however, sharpened awareness of the environment at the same time as they manipulated the way in which reality appeared. Photographs recorded not physical reality but a visible aspect before a lens interpreted by the light and elements of composition chosen by the photographer.

The projection of images by means of the *camera obscura* dates back hundreds of years. In the fifteenth century Leonardo da Vinci described the process and how artists could use it to gain perspective and reduce the size of large objects. Eighteenth-century chemists found methods to preserve images on leather and resins. In the same century silhouettists perfected their art, making at least one type of portrait available to clients of modest means. In 1786 Gilles-Louis Chrétien invented the *physiontrace*, a device that exactly copied facial outlines. William Hyde Wollaston, an Englishman, intro-

duced his *camera lucida* in 1807, an improved technique for projecting images. Finally, in France in 1826, Joseph Nicéphore Niépce (1765–1833) used chemically coated metal exposed to light to produce an image. The exposure took eight hours and was taken from a window in Niépce's home. The result was epochal, and it ultimately revolutionized the graphic arts.[9] Unable to find ready commercial uses for his discovery, the inventor formed a partnership with Louis Jacques Mandé Daguerre (1787–1851), a scenic painter and amateur scientist. In 1837, four years after Niépce's death, Daguerre perfected a way to fix the photographic image using a chemical, hyposulfite of soda, or "hypo." This was the first widely applicable photographic process: modern photography was born. Few inventions so quickly reached an excited public, and fewer still had so vast an impact on the ways in which society saw itself.

Daguerre's technique, announced at a joint meeting of the French Academies of Sciences and of Fine Arts in August 1839, produced no negatives and was cumbersome. The competition to find a way to create a permanent photographic image was fierce, and more or less at the same time, at least three other scientists independently discovered similar processes. They were William Henry Fox Talbot (1800–1877) in England, using paper negatives (the calotype); a Frenchman, Hippolyte Bayard (1801–1877), who exhibited thirty photographs made by a paper-chemical process in 1839; and Antoine Hercules Romauld Florence (1804–1879), a French immigrant residing in the Brazilian town of Vila São Paulo (today Campinas in São Paulo state).[10]

Fox Talbot, who was a member of the landed gentry and an inveterate inventor, patented his discovery in 1840 in London after revealing it to the British Royal Society. But he was upstaged by the French. That government purchased Daguerre's patent, awarded him the Legion of Honour, pensioned him off, and made the secret freely available to the world as a grand gesture of French achievement. Daguerre's seventy-nine page description of his process was published within two years in more than thirty cities around the world. Fox Talbot's images were grainier and less sharp than the metallic daguerreotypes, and to use his method one had

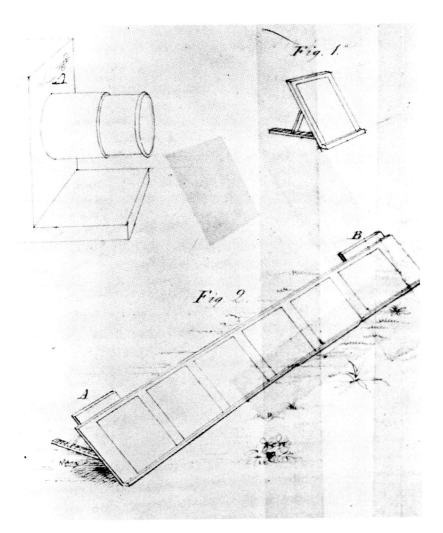

1.1 H. Florence Sketch of "Photographic Devices," BK

to pay permission to the patent holder. As a result, the lustrous, silvery daguerreotypes dominated the first generation of photography even though each individual image was unique and could not be reproduced.

Hercules Florence's story demonstrates the frustrations of pre-twentieth-century Latin Americans attempting to join the mainstream of Western science and culture, and the distance, psychological and real, between Latin America and Europe. Fox Talbot's and Daguerre's processes were discovered independently by Florence several years earlier in Brazil, but that fact remains a footnote to photographic history.[11]

The son of a surgeon in Bonaparte's army, Florence had trained in physics, mathematics, and art in his youth, but he became discontented with prospects at home. Invited to Brazil by a ship captain who was a family friend, he arrived in Rio de Janeiro in 1824 after a six-week voyage from Europe. After a year working at odd jobs he answered a newspaper advertisement seeking an artist to join a scientific expedition headed by the Russian consul, Baron von Langsdorff, and sponsored by Czar Alexander I. As "second draftsman," Florence spent four

years in the jungle interior with the troupe of botanists, astronomers, naturalists, and their slave carriers covering over 13,000 kilometers before returning to Rio de Janeiro in 1829. His more than 200 paintings and drawings were sent to St. Petersburg where they were stored in the Hermitage. He then married a Brazilian woman he had met at the outset of the expedition and settled down.

Seeking to publish some of his observations from his journeys, but frustrated by the fact that there was only one printing press in São Paulo at that time, he set out to experiment with printing methods. In 1830 he developed a kind of mimeograph system, which he called *polygraphie*. His method did not prove commercially successful, and in 1832 he turned to experiments seeking, in the words of his diary, to find chemical substances that would react in the presence of light. Early in 1833 he wrote of his work with a negative-positive process using silver nitrate supplied to him by a pharmacist, Joaquim Correia de Mello. In January 1833 Florence wrote the following entry in his diary:

I decided to draw on a glass pane 'à la

manière naturelle.' I will take a copy with sunlight on another glass pane previously covered by me with a layer of silver nitrate . . . there will be the drawing, but in such a way that the white tones will appear in place of the darks, and vice versa . . . I will then put sheets of paper under this glass and will have the copies from nature (au naturel).[12]

Florence's diaries show drawings of cameras and printing frames, and contain detailed chemical formulae and descriptions of his work with light-sensitive substances. Fox Talbot discovered virtually the same process six years later. Florence named his process *photographie*. But he was cautious not to describe his work at length publicly, because he feared that it would be stolen. More concerned with finding a way to copy drawings than to work from nature, he actually succeeded in reproducing medicine labels and Masonic certificates. Then he moved on to other projects. In the end his efforts to earn recognition for his work gained him little more than a brief statement published in the São Paulo newspaper, *A Phenix*, in October 1839 and reprinted in Rio de Janeiro's *Jornal do*

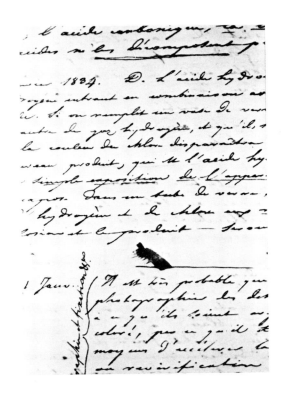

Comercio in December of that year.

Florence remained self-conscious about his isolation. He grew annoyed as one after another of his "near-inventions" was perfected and then manufactured elsewhere; it is not known to what extent he attempted to press his claims as photography's inventor beyond Brazil. Two letters sent by Florence to the French Academy

through the French chargé in Rio de Janeiro went unanswered. Had the inventor journeyed back to France things may well have been different, although Daguerre's fame, and the role of the French government in solidifying it, had quickly become a very powerful obstacle.[13]

From the outset daguerreotypists followed French artistic convention, which in the 1840s combined romanticism with mannered classicism, the goal being to tell a simple story in an aesthetically pleasing way, emphasizing pictorial exactitude. "The resultant realism and literalness were welcomed by a public who knew little of art," Robert Sobieszek reminds us, "the same public who had greeted photography enthusiastically."[14] Photographers who worked in Latin America came to be rewarded for emphasizing the cosmopolitan appearance of elite urban life. The camera permitted the "better classes," as they were known, to show off their finery and cultivated European patina. Photographers who understood the wishes of their clientele were more likely to prosper. Photography in Latin America came to emphasize images of the picturesque (the poor, the exotic), the important (the affluent), and the beautiful (European).[15]

Daguerreotypes

In spite of the link between art and photography, the early photographers considered themselves scientists, not artists. Socially they fit roughly into the middle of the Latin American status hierarchy—higher than manual workers and most tradesmen, but not as high as businessmen, who, mostly foreign-born themselves, ranked below Creoles from the better families.[16] Photographers were aware of artistic convention and sought to use their bulky and primitive cameras to curb nature and bring it in line with tradition. In portraiture daguerreotypists were constrained by the fact that long exposures made sitting an ordeal. But clients still flocked to the studios; illustrated magazines, which began to reproduce daguerreotypes through the use of wood engravings and other methods, witnessed an instant demand for portraits of celebrities.[17]

Early nature daguerreotypy emphasized the *juste milieu*, and approached the outdoors as if it were an extension of the studio. Travel books published in the first half of the nineteenth century were often illustrated by tableaux so seemingly realistic that to us they look like lithographs taken from photographs. In fact, it was the other way around: daguerreotypists (and their photographer descendants) borrowed the artist's compositional eye.[18]

The daguerreotypists were limited by technology. Their materials were not sensitive enough to record nuance: rippling water, wisps of smoke, figures moving at their normal pace —all went unrecorded. But daguerreotypes were accepted as topographical documents and were used by naturalists, explorers, and travelers throughout the continent. Daguerreotypes taken outdoors required sharper lenses than those used for portraits, where speed was the critical factor, and used mirrors or prisms to reverse the composed image. Itinerant daguerreotypists used team-drawn wagon studios and set up shop in vacant lots or in public squares. The first daguerreotypist in the Americas, D. W. Seager, received Daguerre's published instructions on the process from Samuel F. B. Morse, who brought it from Paris. Seager went on to Mexico. A few years later he gave up photography to become an agricultural advisor to the Juárez government in the 1860s.[19]

The daguerreotypists, of course, could only reproduce still images, like buildings or human subjects frozen into hardened poses. They also sought images that appeared artistically composed: symmetrical plantings or reflections in water.[20] Torn between their self-images as scientist/naturalists on one hand and an awareness of artistic rules on the other, and further limited by their equipment, the daguerreotypists attempted to do both. As a result they produced photographs which appear awkward and artificial to us. Yet their potential fired the imagination. Delaroche, seeing a daguerreotype for the first time in 1839, was said to remark that "from today, painting is dead."

News of the daguerreotype process arrived in Latin America coincident with a surge in urban growth and the emergence of a national consciousness. Readers of *El Observador* in Bogotá, *Correo de Caracas*, and *El Comercio* in Lima were given detailed accounts of the Fox Talbot and Daguerre discoveries in September of 1839, only one month after Daguerre's fame was acclaimed in Paris and four months after *Blackwood's Edinburgh Magazine* had described the process. Rio de Janeiro's *Jornal do Comercio* published an article about daguerreotypy on May 1, 1839,

three months *before* the invention's official announcement in Paris.[21]

A French abbot, Louis Compte, demonstrated the process in Rio de Janeiro in January 1840, reproducing and showing the first publicly acknowledged photochemical images in South America. This was only three months after the process was demonstrated for the first time in New York City by D. W. Seager. Father Compte arrived in Brazil at the port of Salvador on the school *corvée L'Orientale*, which was sailing around the world with Belgian and French students and their science tutors. Among the vessel's equipment was a physiontrace "for studying races" and Daguerre's machine.

Compte may have created daguerreotype prints in Salvador, but Rio de Janeiro, the imperial capital, came away with the recognition. Compte produced a small number of daguerreotypes of the city's public buildings, including a view of the Largo de Paço, which was described in a story in the *Jornal do Comercio* in January (1.3). The image is unusual for its inclusion, at such an early date, of standing figures on two levels of the church. The long vantage point compresses the adjacent buildings and conveys the image of urban density. Because the human figures are so tiny, nearly requiring a magnifying glass to be seen, the daguerreotype image seems depopulated; there is virtually no sense of the normal bustling activity which usually filled the plaza. But the likeness, which achieves a certain three-dimensionality because of the rocky terrain in the lower right portion of the image, is nonetheless striking.

The exhibition of Compte's daguerreotypes provoked great excitement. The fifteen-year-old emperor, Pedro II, a budding patron of the arts and sciences, requested a private demonstration of the daguerreotype. He immediately purchased a camera, for 250 *mil-réis,* making him probably the first Brazilian to make daguerreotypes.[22] In February 1840 *L'Orientale* sailed to Montevideo, where its arrival created such excitement that some Argentines braved a naval blockade of their port to cross over into Uruguay. The ship was to make its next call at Buenos Aires but it could not land owing to "political upheaval." After sailing through the Straits of Magellan, *L'Orientale* was wrecked off the coast of Valparaiso. All aboard were rescued but the school ship venture abruptly ended.[23]

1.3 Compte, Largo do Paço, GF

Compte had remained in Montevideo, but his camera went down with the ship.

Within months of Compte's visit others began to work in the photographic medium. A second view of Brazil's royal city palace dates from 1842, showing the arrival of a carriage attended by more than two dozen mounted soldiers, onlookers, and a second level of shops and residences stretching in the distance (1.4). The photographer was Augustus Morand, a Frenchman. According to the Reverend Daniel Kidder, an American resident of Brazil at the time, Morand prepared for his photograph by setting up his cameras and plates in advance, since the emperor visited his city palace every Saturday. Kidder noted that the photographer developed his plate, dried it, framed it, and presented it to the young emperor all within forty minutes of the exposure. His equipment provided a maximum aperture of about f 14—primitive by modern standards but adequate to reproduce fixed subjects in good light.[24]

The resulting images were significant improvements on the first daguerreotypes. Focusing at a shorter distance than Compte had done two years earlier, Morand produced an altogether different kind of composition in which the buildings dwarfed the people and horses standing below. Some of the figures in the foreground remain as semitransparent ghosts, but the scene takes on life because of the presence of animate subjects.

Daguerreotype portraits were instantly popular among those who could afford them. Beaumont Newhall describes them: "(S)ilvered copper plates were polished mirror bright; fumed straw yellow and rose red with vapors of iodine, chlorine and bromine; exposed in bulky wooden cameras; developed over heated mercury; fixed, gilded, washed, and fitted like jewels in cases."[25]

The portraits were available in a number of sizes, with the largest (6½ by 8½ inches) requiring an exposure ten times longer than the smallest. A popular fixing process invented in 1840 using gold chloride gave deep, warm tones to the image, and many of the early portraits were hand colored, a delicate operation involving application of individual dots of paint and stencils.[26] A student at the São Paulo Law Academy wrote to his mother: "The daguerreotype is the latest fashion here. There is no student who hasn't had his portrait done. . . . After all, it is cheap; for a small amount we can get a small coloured portrait in a simple frame. But not only students have caught the daguerreotype disease; the malady has spread to the professors themselves."[27] His reference to the use of color is a reminder that photographic portraitists still treated their images as paintings. We can assume that the fees were high, but law students (and professors) in the nineteenth century came from the moneyed sectors of society. The loyalty of these elites to traditional artists permitted the survival of portrait painting as an art form for the rich; but as time passed, even the best portraitists based their work on photographs as well as formal sittings.

Travelers affiliated with the French diplomatic corps were among the first to import photographic equipment to Latin America. In New Granada French Ambassador Baron Jean-Baptiste Louis Gros, who was a naturalist and painter, experimented with Daguerre's methods as soon as they were announced. His earliest work (possibly the world's first photographic landscapes) did not survive; but we do have a

1.4 Attributed to Morand, Paço da Cidade, 1842, GF

view of Bogotá's Calle del Observatorio dated 1842 (1.5). Exposure time was forty-seven seconds, too long to include human figures; but the result offers a remarkable view of the mountain city, then boasting less than 50,000 inhabitants and buffeted by the economic dislocations brought about by nearly continuous war.

The image captures the social distinctions in mid-nineteenth-century Latin American urban centers. Two-story dwellings belonging to wealthy landowners and businessmen—their balconies attesting to the social standing of their owners and the seclusion of upper-class women—abut squat, single-story houses owned by or rented to master artisans and other members of the middle sectors. Both types of dwelling stand side by side, unprotected from the easily flooded, unpaved streets with their open sewers. Bogotá was not yet divided into neighborhoods based on wealth or status. The street is narrow, a legacy of colonial urban legislation based on the premise that streets were passageways, not centers of social activity.[28]

In the next few years Daguerre's process established itself throughout Latin American cities. A daguerreotype studio opened on Rio's

Rua d'Ouvidor in 1840. A French photographer, Maximiliano Danti, opened a studio in Lima sometime in 1841. This was at least a month before the first photographic studio opened in Berlin, always one of the earliest cities to sample scientific novelties. In London Richard Beard, a coal merchant and part-time inventor, obtained patent rights from Daguerre and opened a portrait studio in March 1841.[29] A Frenchman in Caracas who called himself "Monsieur Antoine" opened a combination daguerreotype gallery and pistol shop in 1845. A daguerrotypist named Francisco Goñíz may have established a portrait studio in that same city a year or two before that.

Daguerreotypes were exhibited at the Brazilian Imperial Academy in 1845 under royal patronage. The Academy had been established under the tutelage of a French cultural mission in 1816, and its directors were eager to reassert the Franco-Brazilian artistic link. Daguerreotype studios opened in Salvador, in the interior city of Ouro Preto, and in Recife by 1845. The sitting process was uncomfortable and tedious: slow lenses permitted no movement at all; heads had to be held fast by metal clamps, as in the portrait of the young Brazilian emperor, Pedro II (1.6).

A North American, Charles Elliot, established a portraiture studio in Buenos Aires in mid-1843, charging one hundred pesos for a framed daguerreotype.[30] One of the earliest daguerreotypists to travel from the United States to Latin America was another American, Charles De Forest Fredricks. He was the pupil (and after 1856, the partner) of New York's leading daguerreotypist, Jeremiah Gurney, a jeweler from Saratoga, New York, who opened a daguerreotype studio in 1840. Fredricks was sent by his family to Havana to learn Spanish before he finished high school. In 1843, at twenty, he sailed to Venezuela, but customs officials refused to permit him to enter Angostura (now Ciudad Bolívar) with his equipment. Fredricks was hosted by a prominent merchant whose son died during the visit. To permit Fredricks to make a daguerreotype of the dead child, he used his influence to liberate the impounded equipment. Within three weeks Fredricks had exhausted his materials and earned $4,000.

Fredricks then returned to New York for more chemicals, later returning to South Amer-

1.6 Anonymous, Pedro II with head in clamp, GF

1.7 Bennet, Daguerreotype of J. Montoya, ES
1.8 Anonymous, Daguerreotype of E. Pérez, ES

ica and traveling with his brother up the Orinoco River to Brazil and down the Amazon, "daguerreotyping all the way." At the Mapuera rapids Indian guides ran away with the canoes and provisions; Fredricks and his brother waited twenty-two days for rescue, living on sour manioc.[31] In 1844 Fredricks went back to Latin America and remained for nine years, working his way south from Belém. While traveling through Rio Grande do Sul in southern Brazil, en route to Montevideo and Buenos Aires, he traded a horse for each portrait; at the end of his trip, accompanied by "an immense drove of horses," he sold them for three dollars each.[32] The governor of Corrientes gave him a live puma in exchange for a daguerreotype portrait.[33] He remained in the Plata area for another year, then went to Paris to study the new glass-plate process. His firm opened a branch in Havana in 1855, and he visited it for a while although hired assistants presumably did all of the photography.[34]

Relatively more urban and cosmopolitan than the rest of Latin America, the southern nations of South America provided receptive ground

1.9 Anonymous, Daguerreotype of Simona de Botero, ES

1.10 Anonymous, Daguerreotype of Juan y Josefa Sordo, ES

1.11 Price, Self-portrait with Hevia, ES

for the establishment of photographic businesses. Many firms were established, and by the middle 1840s thriving portrait studios existed in every major city in the Americas.[35] Three English brothers, the Helsbys, opened a daguerreotype studio in Santiago, Chile, in 1843. Within a few years several studios opened in Santiago and Valparaiso.[36]

The first studio in then backwater São Paulo opened in 1851. Rio de Janeiro, close to the imperial residence in Petrópolis and the port of entry for most commerce, became the major Brazilian center for photography. Fredricks, soon to own the largest commercial photographic establishment in the United States, operated a major gallery in partnership with Alexander B. Weeks.[37] The accounting records of the imperial court reveal large outlays to photographers.[38] In the European tradition photographers who at some point were hired to photograph a member of the royal family (in Brazil), or the president or chief of state, included the distinction in their subsequent advertising.

The portrait of the Duke of Caxias illustrates the ways in which early photographers used props to embellish their subjects (1.12). The goal was to imitate painted portraits of European royalty, a convention which lasted into the 1870s in Latin America. Caxias, an imperial nobleman and the commander-in-chief of the Brazilian Army, not only wears a plumed, full-dress uniform but is posed against a tapestry backdrop selected to suggest regal elegance. He stands stiffly, as if propped up by the short pillar, with the air of a stuffed museum exhibit.

As elsewhere, the first daguerreotypists in Rio de Janeiro were foreigners—Conrad Geibig from Germany, Augustus Morand from France, the Swiss Louis Abraham Buvelot, and Americans W. R. Williams, J. D. Davis, and Henry Schmidt. An Irish magician, Frederick Walter—like a character from a García Márquez novel—incorporated daguerreotypy into his traveling magic act across the interior of the Brazilian province of Ceará.[39] But in spite of the excitement the daguerreotypists produced, many failed as businessmen. Few stayed in one place; they moved frequently from one location to another, sometimes selling their equipment

before departing but usually taking their bulky cameras with them. The career of John Armstrong Bennet typifies this pattern. An Alabaman whose first studio was in Mobile, Bennet traveled to Buenos Aires in the mid-1840s, moved to Montevideo, then to Bogotá where he stayed two years (1849 to 1851), finally selling out to an Englishman named Henry Price, only to return again for another eight years.[40] The most prominent daguerreotypist in Medellín was Emílio Herbruger, a German who operated galleries in Cuba, then Mexico, then Central America, the United States, and finally New Granada, where he settled permanently, turning over his studios in Bogotá, Medellín, Cali, and Panama to his son.[41]

Unreliable equipment frustrated the early daguerreotypists. The first cameras with accessories weighed fifty kilograms, or more than one hundred pounds. Plates had to be exposed to toxic mercury fumes. Preparation time for each photograph took up to forty-five minutes with additional time for exposure of the plate. Sunlight or bright shade was mandatory; when it rained, or when the sun went down, photographers hooded their lenses. Results were un-

1.12 Duke of Caxias, GF

even at best. Customers found that some of their prized daguerreotypes faded or "evaporated."[42]

The instructions provided by Daguerre for his process were imprecise, forcing individual photographers to improvise. Some of the early daguerreotypists were either amateur photographers who soon returned to their original occupations, or were get-rich-quick merchants who moved on, selling their equipment to others. Cameras still were not trusted. Many portraitists adopted the daguerreotype, but only to fix an image intended as the model for a painted portrait.

Within a few short years technological advances revolutionized photography. Many of the new developments were pioneered in the United States; at the 1851 Crystal Palace Exhibition in London, North Americans took three of the five medals in daguerreotyping.[43] Calotypes derived from the Fox Talbot process improved in quality and could be duplicated from negatives stored in the photographer's studio. Camera size and weight shrunk, and prices of equipment fell by thirty or forty percent. By 1846 annual camera sales in Paris reached two thou-sand, and a half-million pre-treated photographic plates were sold to the French public.[44]

Daguerreotypes became obsolete rapidly. With the freeing of restrictions on the Talbot method in 1853, and rapid technical advances, by 1855 only a handful of professional photographers in Europe still used Daguerre's process, although the numbers were higher in Latin America.[45] By 1860 both the daguerreotype and the calotype were supplanted by portraits taken using the wet-plate process of collodion-on-glass negatives, invented by the Englishman Frederick Scott Archer in 1851. It combined the daguerreotype's clarity of detail and grainless-ness with the calotype's reproducibility, producing what was commercially called an *ambrotype*.[46] These and other developments significantly broadened photographers' markets. Ambrotypes had greater compositional range and hence greater potential for spontaneity. Yet by the end of the daguerreotype period, some lensmen had achieved a remarkable level of skill. The image of a slave woman in front of her hut in the province of Rio de Janeiro was taken in 1857 using a daguerreotype camera (1.13); the group of four young men and the street scene of Recife in 1860 are both ambrotypes (figs. 1.14, 1.15).

For a time daguerreotypists coexisted with the photographers that were using the more versatile negative processes. From about 1860 coated papers could be purchased in a prepared state (coated but still not sensitized). These were stained in gold tone, which later faded to sepia, to give them a permanence not previously attainable. Smaller cameras with more versatile lenses appeared at about the same time, bringing the trade to a new level. Exposure times dropped to thirteen minutes by 1840, to two or three minutes by 1841, to twenty to fifty seconds by 1842. By the end of the 1840s exposures were reduced to a few seconds at most.

Only a tiny portion of the first photographic images manufactured in Latin America survive. Since daguerreotypes could not be duplicated, studios amassed no file collections of them. Individual prints were costly, and proprietors rarely produced more than one exposure at a sitting. Daguerreotype portraits were handed down from generation to generation within families, but many faded or were lost, damaged, or eventually discarded. Few of the works

1.13 Christiano Júnior, Woman in front of hut, FN

attributed to the pioneering American photographer Charles Fredricks, from his decade of photographic travels across South America, have ever been found.

Members of the "classes altas" were so eager to preserve their likenesses on the silver-plated copper daguerreotype plates that they paid hefty prices not only for their portraits but for cases inlaid with mother-of-pearl, semiprecious stones, and gold. In 1850 the least expensive daguerreotype portrait in Colombia cost ten Grenadine pesos, and one could spend up to twenty for hand-colored images richly framed. One peso was the average monthly wage for a cook or a seamstress; it cost between 400 and 1,500 pesos to construct a house in an upper-class district.[47]

Even if the daguerreotypists were responsible for little work of permanence, by working in upper-class circles they managed to make family photographs a part of urban culture. The advantage of the daguerreotype was that it was less expensive than paintings. The Ecuadorian miniaturist Antonio Santos Zevallos, who ran a Lima studio in the 1840s, charged twenty-five Peruvian pesos plus the cost of the frame.

London-born Balthazar R. Herve, who used a cameralike device to reproduce the subject's silhouette, which he painted, charged between seven and twelve pesos, plus the frame. Maximiliano Danti charged only six pesos, and the fee included framing.[48]

Of the Europeans who introduced photography to Latin America, Germans, Englishmen, and Frenchmen predominated, joined by displaced nationals from Italy, Central Europe, and Spain. In the next generation Latin American–born photographers established themselves alongside a small but steady flow of newcomers from overseas. Some, like the Brazilian-born Marc Ferrez, were trained in Europe.

These early photographers, as their artist predecessors, were uninterested in experimentation in technical areas and did not seek to establish their own photographic style; they were content to imitate fashions and practices imported from abroad. Even after the turn of the century few outlets for artistic or "creative" photographs emerged. Worldwide the growing profession continued to be characterized by strongly preserved colonial attitudes: the further North American and European photogra-

1.14 Four young men, ES

1.15 Recife street scene, 1860, GF

phers journeyed to bring back images, the more they seemed to emphasize the exotic, the antiquarian, and the quaint.

Within two months of the announcement of the discovery of photography in 1839, two French daguerreotypists traveled to Egypt to record the pyramids. Felix Beato, an English photographer who had started in Egypt and India, worked in Japan in the mid-1860s producing hand-colored photographs of "native type(s) often carried to garish extremes."[49] Latin American elites cringed when they saw photographs of their own countries taken in this way. They did everything that could be done to guarantee that views of their societies would emphasize the stately, the orderly, and the civilized. The glamour and excitement of photography's early decades had faded. Photographers were now businessmen working within a limited and highly conservative marketplace. Photographers who were able to transcend these restraints and who managed to develop individual compositional styles merit praise for what they accomplished, not condemnation for what they could not.

1.16 Studio of Jean-Baptiste Louis Gros, ES

Chapter two examines the evolving reciprocal relationship in Latin America between photography and elite behavior—a relationship that is sharply illustrated by the way that dominant groups, prompted by the values of an urbanizing society, used photography to augment methods of social control. It also considers the

reasons why Latin American documentary photography developed in promising ways but ultimately failed to branch out into new and assertive forms, as occurred in the United States and in Western Europe.

Developments in technique and style

THE INFLUENCE of Daguerre's "magic box" was eclipsed in the 1850s with the arrival of processes that yielded paper negatives and glass plates. Collodion or wet-plate photographs, ambrotypes, and tintypes permitted photographic images to be duplicated and even improved in the darkroom for the first time. Europe and North America witnessed an explosion of new styles and motifs as photographers packed up their equipment and ventured beyond their studios—slowly at first, in part because of the legal necessity to pay royalties on every photograph taken.

In most of Latin America the second half of the nineteenth century was characterized by physical change in the human environment accompanied by economic laissez-faire and social conservatism. Now swollen in size as a result of commercial and industrial growth and migration from impoverished rural zones, Latin American cities continued to be dominated by the conservative and hidebound social institutions of the past. The neo-colonial climate did not encourage the removal of barriers to up-ward mobility. This atmosphere, in which large portions of the citizenry remained illiterate and unskilled, militated against the development of magazines, mass-circulation newspapers, and other vehicles which elsewhere offered opportunities for photographers.

There are conflicting views regarding photographers' possibilities in this environment. Keith McElroy, a specialist on nineteenth-century Peru, contends that it was photography's lack of binding traditions and formal aesthetic that appealed to contemporary practitioners. As the earliest of the "technological media," photography promised a "perfect wedding of aesthetics and social aspirations."[1] It thrived in Latin America not only because the elites were predisposed to applied science but also because the new field permitted them to compete as equals with Europeans, since it was so new and so unencumbered by tradition.

What emerged from the nineteenth-century convention that photographic images were "natural" or relics of nature, was a pseudo-objective, neutral documentary style. Photographers were content to remain within the safe boundaries of publicly approved subjects: archi-tecture, portraits, landscapes, still lifes, curiosities. The first offshoot from daguerreotype portraitists were the view photographers who sought images to sell to editors of travel books published abroad. Most came from the ranks of portraitists; they continued to divide their time between their studios and outdoors.[2] The increased technical flexibility among these photographers yielded a range of styles: some began to specialize in images of monuments and architecture, others in pastoral landscapes, and still others in views of natives in local costume. But sales, in contrast to the situation in Europe and North America, remained very limited. Worse, photographers in Latin America were pulled in two directions: local elites wanted conventional portraits and reproductions of public works and monuments, while foreign buyers sought exotic vistas and curiosities.

The advent of new opportunities for photographic expression in the second half of the nineteenth century coincided with the adoption of French positivism by most of Latin America's ruling classes. Positivism, whose motto was "Order and Progress," was the major ideology

of political, economic, and social life. It coun-
seled that societies should be governed by pater-
nal elites who secure material progress through
imposed law and order and should accept economic dependency as the cost of cheap imports
and foreign investment. The positivist ideology
extolled scientific particularism, materialism,
and naturalism. Emphasizing the behavorial
study of nature and social objects, positivists
expected artists to see nature in exactly the same
way as the scientist, suppressing personal sub-
jectivity in the interest of finding objective reality in material nature.[3]

The strength of positivism in mid-nineteenth-
century Latin America may have dampened enthusiasm for experimentation with new ways of
portraying subjects. To be sure, its impact varied from country to country, and some places
experienced little impact at all. Nonetheless,
photographic poses tended to be the same not
only throughout Latin America but around the
world. This was due to the technical capabilities
(and limitations) of the industry and the commercial constraints on the artistic pretensions of
photographers.

Customers tended to be satisfied with stock
poses. Portraits remained in demand, and daguerreotypes still served customers' purposes.
Affluent customers paid to have their studio
portraits hand colored, making compositions at
once strangely true to life and dreamlike.[4] The
major technical transition came in the early
1860s, when *carte de visite* technology became
widespread. The mass-produced *cartes*—called
tarjetas de visita in Spanish-speaking countries
—were cheap and fast. As a result, they made
photographs suddenly available to a much
broader spectrum of the population, although
in Latin America potential customers remained
a relatively small group in comparison with
Europe and North America.

The *carte de visite* was patented in Paris in
1854 by a Frenchman of Italian parentage, André
Adolphe E. Disdéri. It did not catch on until
1859, when the Emperor Napoleon III, on his
way to Italy with his army, abruptly detoured to
Disdéri's studio where he sat for his photographic portrait. The whole army, Gisèle
Freund accounts, waited for him in tight formation. The event galvanized Disdéri's fame and
provided his business with a patriotic and democratic image: humble citizens and Napoleon
himself could sit before the same lens.[5] In the
following year Queen Victoria authorized a set
of *carte* portraits of the royal family to be is-
sued. A worldwide craze ensued which lasted
for about a decade: in England alone an estimated several hundred million were sold in the
1860s.[6] The craze spread almost instantly to
Latin America.[7]

The *carte de visite* reached beyond the usual
wealthy clientele to the urban middle class. The
low-priced, mass-produced, full-length portrait
offered eight or ten poses per frame using the
wet-plate process. By shrinking the size of the
individual frames to approximately 2½ by 4
inches, Disdéri was able to lower his prices
from the usual fifty or one hundred francs for a
studio portrait to twenty francs for ten or
twelve photographs. Using a stable of assistants, he provided delivery of the finished photographs in forty-eight hours.

Disdéri and his competitors made their for-
tunes and the profession was transformed.
Within five years millions of *cartes* had been
produced in every major country, with even
small studios manufacturing as many as 6,000
negatives and 50,000 prints annually. People

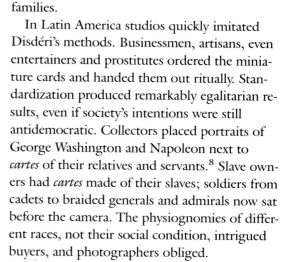

exchanged *cartes*, saved them in special albums, and collected sets of views from all parts of the world. Mass production lowered still further the artistic quality of the results, but in exchange ordinary citizens began to covet photographic records of themselves and their families.

In Latin America studios quickly imitated Disdéri's methods. Businessmen, artisans, even entertainers and prostitutes ordered the miniature cards and handed them out ritually. Standardization produced remarkably egalitarian results, even if society's intentions were still antidemocratic. Collectors placed portraits of George Washington and Napoleon next to *cartes* of their relatives and servants.[8] Slave owners had *cartes* made of their slaves; soldiers from cadets to braided generals and admirals now sat before the camera. The physiognomies of different races, not their social condition, intrigued buyers, and photographers obliged.

The cost of a dozen of the little cardboard-backed portraits was initially about the same as a single daguerreotype, but prices dropped quickly. In 1855 in Buenos Aires five portraits, approximately six by nine or ten centimeters, cost only 100 pesos. As a result, an English observer noted, the low price "enables all of the better middle class" to have their photographs taken. Lacking photographs in daily newspapers, consumers also avidly purchased photographs of statesmen and important events.[9] For the aspiring Latin American bourgeois, trading *tarjetas* became the rage, leading a journalist for Lima's *El Comercio* to complain in 1862 that people were handing out their portraits "as if they were President of the Republic."[10] In Colombia, a war-torn country of fewer than four million inhabitants, an estimated one million *carte*-sized photographs were manufactured in 1886 by several hundred photographers working in its cities and towns.

Once it was apparent that the *carte* format could be successfully adapted to different subjects, photographers redoubled their efforts to capture the exotic. They sensed that these images would sell not only to local buyers but also abroad where interest in the wild and the unusual remained high. Appealing to the wider market did not mean that the photographers needed to stretch the conservative boundaries of conventional taste. After all, the positivist

outlook accepted the commonplace and the everyday as proper objects of study.

When ethics came up against business, commercialism prevailed. Photographers posed slaves, Indians, nonwhites, and the poor in ways which emphasized their colorfulness and lent to them a kind of artificial, attributed dignity. The young woman in 2.2a sits stiffly, one hand resting on an improbable umbrella, the other on a table decorated with a potted plant. She is dressed in a billowing skirt, and is wearing a small necklace. In daily life she was still a slave, a fact which remains apparent in the photograph.[11] More "respectable" sitters tended to project their emotions more. A young Mexican mother proudly holds her child in a *carte* which she gave to her family and friends (2.2b).

The *cartes* lent themselves to other applications as well. Political figures ordered thousands of their portraits for distribution to the public. Photographers sold *cartes* of celebrities, monuments, performers, local "types," and religious images; some sold "art" scenes, including tastefully draped nudes. It is not known whether a nineteenth-century version of pornographic *cartes* ever was manufactured or sold, but European photographers started the practice at least by the early 1860s, and undoubtedly some were imported to Latin America from abroad.

Consumerism broadened the photographic market in several directions. In the 1860s individual firms began to experiment with enlargements, using such devices as the solar camera, a primitive enlarger which produced pale images which were then painted by artists—a method very popular in the United States.[12] New processes permitted larger photographs than the tiny *carte* size: by the early 1870s, in fact, the introduction of the cabinet photograph (typically 6½ by 4¼ inches) permitted far more satisfying individual and group portraits than the *cartes* and became the standard until after 1900.[13] Shopkeepers imported special photograph albums, picture frames, and studio backdrops. Some albums were manufactured in rich leather or satin, lavishly decorated with silver- or gold-embossed designs—middle-class versions of the gilded and bejeweled daguerreotype frames fashionable among the rich in the 1840s and 1850s. Some were equipped with built-in music boxes imported from Switzerland or Germany. By the 1860s the public began to

2.2b Mexican woman and child, UNM

pay more to have photographs retouched. Some portraits were reduced in size and mounted as photojewelry or placed in tiny lockets.

Such inventions spawned subgroups of artisans and craftsmen, some employed by photographic studios, others working independently. Both art and photography during these years followed the precept that the role of the portraitist was to recreate nature, taking advantage of light, perspective, and shadow and emphasizing physical details. But styles began to change. Studios in large cities abandoned the portrait style that imitated paintings of European royalty—the early model for provincial portrait artists in Latin America—and posed subjects more naturally, permitting the subject's personality to come through.[14]

The enduring worldwide portrait mania encouraged some diversification in poses, but mostly along traditional lines. Photographers asked their subjects to project their character by doing one thing or another with their arms or legs, even encouraging them to clown before the camera.[15] Photographers manufactured more and more images of "typical" or exotic figures from society—water carriers, "savage Indians," old men and women, beggars, child prodigies. In a way the photographer was simply performing the same function as the early nineteenth-century *costumbristas*, recording interesting "types" as objects of curiosity. Positivism's interest in this kind of scientific inventory-taking made the transition from art to photography even smoother.

The practice of recording life in the street was somewhat paralleled in Britain by the efforts of Fox Talbot, John Thompson, Cuban-born Peter Henry Emerson, and others who set out with cameras to document the London poor and rural life in the provinces. These British documentary photographers set about their tasks systematically, capturing with their lenses the down-and-out Londoners that middle-class folk saw daily but ignored. Thompson's photographic books gave faces to the invisible poor and provided a prereform sense of social contrasts. Emerson's photographs of rural East Anglia sought to capture nostalgically a vanished agricultural world.[16]

By contrast, the Latin American *carte de visite* and cabinet-sized snapshots of lower-class people were produced without explicit editorial context. Images sold to foreign tourists and to illustrate books printed abroad emphasized local color; Latin American citizens preferred stately portraits and scenes extolling progress. There was no conflict: foreign-born and local photographers manufactured all kinds of images on demand.

Photography remained a rite for the affluent and a vehicle by which to hold at arm's distance the poor, the unfamiliar, and the nonconforming. The most prevalent theme in the photographs produced during the period from the 1840s through the 1880s was "taming the wilderness"; that is, they documented the ways in which imported technology and modern values were transforming the continent. Thousands and perhaps tens of thousands of photographs were commissioned of railroads, port facilities, urban construction, public utilities, new avenues and boulevards—explicit images to convey the message that Latin America was joining the modern world.

Meanwhile, photographers cast about for new merchandising opportunities. New photographic novelties offered for sale included multiple images on single prints, and the so-called

Rembrandt effect in which portraits were illuminated by strong side light.[17] Odd-shaped frames, embossed print holders, tinted finishes, and a host of other variations were used by photographic studios to distinguish their finished product from competitors' and to appeal to the tastes of the general public. As time passed photographers began to use natural, outdoor sites as background, although poses were kept controlled. The public still expected portraits of "proper" men and women to be dignified and lacking in spontaneity.[18]

By the last third of the century cameras had become sufficiently simple that photographers no longer needed to be craftsmen or chemists: they were technicians. Photographic workshops were no longer costly to equip. Photographers began to use their cameras for architectural surveys, for medical uses, in journalism, and in advertising. Professionals switched from non-reproducible metal plates to wet plates, producing negatives of glass, paper, and ultimately celluloid.

Glass and paper allowed photographers to build up inventories of their shots. Juan Fuentes, the first Peruvian-born photographer to create a successful business, charged customers for taking their portraits and then sold them the negatives, demonstrating how to develop them. In 1858 Fuentes petitioned the government to hire him to photograph criminals, runaways, public officials, and soldiers and to maintain a photographic inventory of public buildings. Although this had been done since the 1840s in Europe (adopted in Switzerland in 1842 and in Britain two years later) and in the United States, the proposal was not adopted. Officials endorsed the petition but rejected it on the grounds of cost. A judge raised the point that such a photographic rogues' gallery could infringe on the rights of individuals by tarnishing the reputation of persons arrested for suspected crimes.[19] Ultimately, Fuentes was hired by prison officials to take mug shots of prison inmates.

Similar practices were adopted elsewhere. In Uruguay detectives hired photographers to produce composite posters of thieves and convicted murderers for purposes of identification within the police bureau, although at first they forbade public circulation of copies of the composites (figs. 2.3a 2.3b, 2.3c).[20] Photographers now

2.3a Uruguayan criminals, HH

could contribute to the maintenance of "order and progress."

Photography and society

The enthusiasm with which Latin Americans embraced photographic technology reveals how anxious they were to demonstrate their modernity. A combination of insecurity over their status, fascination with science, and underlying

2.3b Uruguayan criminals, HH

fear of the lower classes led urban Latin Americans to reject the slow pace of the rural aristocratic heritage in favor of fast-paced technological change. Photographers came close to botanists and naturalists in their ability to produce a systematic inventory of material culture, and, as long as the optimism of positivism prevailed, society provided adequate if not ample commercial opportunities to photographers.[21]

Although newspapers did not publish photographs for some time, even their descriptions, coupled with public exhibitions, excited readers. An article in Lima's *El Comercio* in March 1840 revealed the first use of a daguerreotype in a French divorce case, the camera having caught the wife's lover lowering himself from her window.[22] Some of the early European photographers using paper negatives, including Fox Talbot, began to produce books of travel scenes. Latin Americans visiting Europe brought them back, and photographs of distant places became instrumental in the education of children, much of which in the nineteenth century was still entrusted to private tutors or to small private

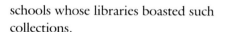

2.3c Mexican criminals, UNM

schools whose libraries boasted such collections.

Many early photographs frustrated their viewers. Unlike the human eye, which is sub-consciously selective, the first photographic images of public places seemed undermined by what Jeffrey terms "telling minutiae," such distracting detail as damaged stonework on majestic ruins or intruding human figures. Science, it seemed, was intruding on art. For one thing, the long exposure times required by the early cameras caused motion to be depicted as blurs, marring the intended "artistic" feeling. Fox Talbot found such distracting items as inscriptions and dates on buildings, advertising placards, or chimney-sweeps interfering with his photographed landscapes of chimneys bordering the horizon.[23]

What likely bothered the public most was the conflict between their idealized visions of reality and the undeniable evidence of the reality itself. Honoré Daumier, the Parisian lithographer and artist, expressed this conflict in his paintings by including street people going about their mundane tasks in counterpoint to the stately presence of public buildings. What Daumier acknowledged deliberately, and the early photographers inadvertently, was the tension between the ideal and the ordinary, between official culture and street life.[24] The early Latin American daguerreotypists did not find this a nagging problem, since their work was done either indoors, in studios, or in the privacy of courtyards and homes. But when they did venture outdoors and become "photographers" they took pains to compose their subjects in ways which would emphasize elegance and symmetry, and they preferred to remove unposed human figures from their field of view. When people did appear they were considered incidental.

August Riedel was a German naturalist who accompanied the Duke of Saxe on wilderness treks during the late 1860s, taking photographs of mines, rivers, and geological sites. Consider his intimately-posed photograph of the slaves and employees of the São João d'El-Rei gold mining corporation in Morro Velho, Minas Gerais (2.4). More than a hundred men and women are crammed into the foreground, separated into groups by sex. The men are dressed in dark jackets and light trousers, presumably denoting their status as technicians, while the women stand in billowing dresses wearing cloth head coverings. An older man with a top hat stands next to a small boy nearest the photographer. Perhaps he is the administrator or chief officer. The scene documents the hierarchy of status and power that was recreated daily in such places, when slaves were counted to see who was unfit for work or who might have escaped.

Cultural norms imported from Catholic Europe to Hispanic America and subject to church scrutiny dominated official life as well as the broader social milieu. Catholicism required uniformity and refused to accept—at least in principle—dissenting or heterodox views.[25] Homogeneity and cultural conformity prevailed, not pluralism. In turn, photographers obeyed the rules and rarely experimented with the ways they portrayed their subjects. Most of the surviving images of nineteenth- and early twentieth-century Latin America reflect this circumstance. Visual images conformed visually to accepted social values. One result was that photographs did not differ very much from country to country. Elites wanted to look European, whether in Montevideo, Guayaquil, or Bogotá. Photographs revealing the underside of everyday life were considered curiosities and usually dismissed.

Traveling European photographers like Frenchman Victor Frond or August Riedel, who came to the New World seeking an inventory of photographs to sell in Europe, viewed the Latin American continent in the same manner as they viewed Africa or China. Their images conveyed the patronizing European belief that backward and primitive societies needed a mixture of western technology and rigid discipline to foster progress. This approach, which was typical of the "white man's burden" theme popular during the nineteenth century, was later taken up by photographers from the United States traveling in Latin America under contract to such firms as Underwood & Underwood, giant photographic clearinghouses specializing in views of scenic and exotic places.

Itinerant foreign photographers did not compete directly with their Latin American counterparts, who tended to remain in their studios taking portraits or to work on assignment for engineering and architectural firms or private

clients. The few early local photographers who specialized in picturesque views always observed conservative conventions, not seeking to challenge the outlook of their audiences. They attempted to convey an air of prosperity and serenity, as in the 1850 photograph of a waterfront neighborhood in Niteroi across the bay from the imperial capital of Rio de Janeiro (2.5). Choice of photographic subject matter was invariably determined by the marketplace. Photographs that sold continued to be those that demonstrated the civilizing presence of human beings and views of luxury, solidity, and cosmopolitan elegance.

Examining the conditions under which photography developed in the urban United States, Peter Bacon Hales argued that artists, scientists, and intellectuals struggled to fit the visual medium into their understanding of the interlocking concepts of art, science, nature, and democracy.[26] In Latin America, democracy was not a consideration. Not until at least 1917 in Mexico, and in most cases not until far later, if at all, did the issue of democratic participation for the masses gain legitimacy. One result of this was that a social-minded documentary tradition, a major and distinct current of photography in Europe and especially in the United States, never emerged in Latin America.

Photographers who recorded unpleasant subjects generally did so under the guise of revealing curious features of life. A "Professor Cotolinger" in Caracas in the 1860s called attention to his illustrated book, *Anales del robo en Venezuela*, by advertising that he had captured on film a case of pickpocketing.[27] Photographs of criminals and victims enjoyed a certain fashionable vogue in the closing years of the nineteenth century, and even in earlier decades photographers such the Caracas-based Frenchman, Henrique Avril, dedicated a portion of their work to images of haggard men, hungry beggars, and famished children. "With regard to Venezuelan photographers during the same period using their cameras as instruments for social change," a modern historian of photography in that country wrote, "we know of none."[28]

One use of photographs in Latin America may have been unique. In the wake of widespread illiteracy and the hazards of travel in areas controlled by individuals or factions hostile to other individuals or factions, versions of *cartes de visite* were distributed as a kind of safe-conduct passport. Survivors of the Brazilian Canudos massacre in 1897 who were permitted to return to the backlands after a period of incarceration, were given *cartes* with the likeness of the repatriation committee's chairman, since he likely would be recognized if the refugees were stopped en route to their villages. In the 1920s the rural bandit chieftain, Lampião, distributed *carte*-sized photographs of himself posing with his rifle to landowners allied with him (and therefore under his protection).[29] Given the fact that nearly 90 percent of the adult population in these locales could neither read nor write during this time, the photographs obviously served as surrogates for written statements.

Photographic images of nineteenth-century Latin America provided an inventory of acceptable attitudes and values. The photographs not only reinforced a nominalist view of social reality but they also made the elite's version of the world manageable. If it is true "that we know about the world if we accept it as the camera records it,"[30] historical photographs and their

daguerreotype ancestors invite speculation and questioning, but within the limits set by the photographers.

The photographers and their world

Even at the height of the photographic boom, when cameramen had refined their techniques and were beginning to cultivate individual creative styles, professional photographers in Latin America retained their initial conservatism. The second generation of photographers were still mostly self-trained freelance businessmen with barely enough capital to buy secondhand equipment and open a studio. Creative artisans were constrained by the marketplace and by the rigid social norms of countries where the affluent strove for material progress within societies configured like pyramids. Elites were neither mean-spirited nor cruel; their behavior was based on the perception that there were two alternatives—society or barbarism—and on altruistic motives rooted in the belief that backwardness could only be overcome by paternalistic modernization. The lower classes, after all, resisted modernization. Progress, the upper

2.6 Rua da Floresta, ca. 1865, GF

classes believed, had to be imposed for the good of all.

The conviction held by most nineteenth-century viewers of photographic images—that incidental details of everyday life marred the artistic value of a print—did not disappear with the passage of time. Photographers who remained in their studios or who visited the homes of the wealthy faced no such paradox; but those who took their lighter and more versatile cameras into the streets or to the countryside continued to wrestle with the disparity between what photographers saw around them and what they were able to photograph. The natural beauty of the landscape evaded their cameras, which reduced the richness of the environment to shades of black and white within a rectangular box measured in millimeters. On the other hand, photographers did not want to show squalor or poverty. Photographs that captured the feeling of a particular place, such as the lush image in 2.6 of a residential intersection in Rio de Janeiro, with human figures and a horse-drawn carriage, were surprisingly rare.

Convention required that Latin American photographers ignore backwardness and pov-

2.7 Cuban nail factory, 1857, HH

erty or that they sanitize it through contrived composition. Some European and North American photographers dealt with the paradox by going in one direction or the other—by turning to more artistic interpretations of their subject matter or by becoming photographic muckrakers. Although photography allowed a fairly good living for the more successful studio owners, few Latin American photographers felt that they had the latitude to venture into the subjective swamps of photographic interpretation. Fewer still were willing to take the risks involved in using the camera for social criticism. Photographers, who were considered tradesmen hardly different from butchers or furniture makers, remained cautious. Especially in the early days of photography, there was no practical reason to take a photograph unless there was reason to believe that it could be sold. We can surmise that Charles De Forest Fredricks had been commissioned to photograph the nail factory in a still rural section of the city of Havana in 1857 (2.7).[31]

The industrialization of photography facilitated its absorption into the bureaucratic workings of society. Photographs came to be used as instruments of social power, as symbolic objects, and as pieces of information. Consider the panorama of Recife's harbor in 1860 (2.8): there is no evidence that as the capital of the depressed sugar region of the Brazilian northeast, the city actually was sliding into decline. The wide-angle lens collapses the commercial buildings into a single handsome line. The rough-hewn *jangada* sailboats which usually plied the harbor are absent. Nor is there evidence of the ragged dockworkers and beggars who frequented the fetid and densely-populated waterside district.

Photographic careers in the postdaguerreotype era followed a general pattern. Photographers maintained the compositional conventions of their predecessors, the naturalistic artists, to the point that some *cartes de visite* are indistinguishable from lithographs produced from line drawings.[32] Invariably, style and specialization set some photographers apart from others. Typical of the more original professionals was Augusto Stahl, who started his career in Recife, Brazil, in 1852. Six years later he moved to the imperial capital, Rio de Janeiro, to open a partnership with a German painter-photographer named Wahnschaffe. Stahl specialized in photographs of ships, complex machinery, and buildings, and sold them to local businesses and banks. He also sold multiple copies of his photographs to foreign engineering and investment firms.

In Colombia Adolphe Duperly, an Anglo-French specialist in views who first worked in Jamaica, sought to photograph the trans-isthmus canal construction project with his son, Henri. But political instability and unsafe conditions in the jungle forced his firm to relocate to Bogotá, where they concentrated on studio portraits, such as the group pose of Army General Staff officers in 2.9.[33]

Most of the images of Brazil sold abroad were taken by foreigners. The republican and anti-Bonapartist Frenchman Victor Frond, who arrived in 1858, was one of the more successful arrivals. His photographs of Latin American architecture were used to produce lithographs which were printed in Paris and which gave Europeans their first systematic glimpse of Latin American life.[34]

There were four Brazilians who specialized in outdoor work in the 1860s and 1870s; but only

2.8 Stahl, Recife, 1859, GF

one, Marc Ferrez (1843–1923), did so exclusively. Ferrez, raised in Brazil but trained in France by the sculptor Alphée Dubois, returned to Rio de Janeiro in about 1859, at the same time that wet collodion plates were introduced from Europe. His father and uncle had come to Brazil in 1816 with the French Artistic Mission, which founded the Brazilian Imperial Academy of Fine Arts. Marc apprenticed with the lithography firm of George Leuzinger in Rio de Janeiro, and ultimately set up his own studio specializing in scenic views, much in the pattern of the European photographers Samuel Bourne, Felix Fonfils, and Francis Frith and the San Francisco-based view photographer Carleton E. Watkins.[35]

Ferrez's photograph of Rio de Janeiro's ferryboat terminal typifies the kind of photographs demanded by his clients. The composition frames the building, not the passersby. The focal point of the photograph, in fact, is the English word "Ferry" under the clock, attesting to the London-based ownership of the steamboat utility. During peak passenger hours the square was filled with hundreds of pedestrians, scurrying to work on the adjacent Rua

2.9 Duperly, Colombian generals and aides, ES

2.10 Ferrez, Ferry terminal, GF

ORDER AND PROGRESS 41

2.11 Ferrez, Docks in Belém do Pará, GF

2.12 Ferrez, Sugar Loaf Mountain, GF

D'Ouvidor or catching a horse-drawn tram (one of them captured in the photograph). But Ferrez's photograph emphasizes the serenity of the scene: the dark-clothed men walk leisurely, as do the black women and children.

Between 1875 and 1900 Ferrez was the predominant Brazilian photographer, at least by today's standards. The harbor scene at dusk in 2.11 is the exception to the rule on conventionality which characterized the work of most of his contemporaries. The semidarkened ships float hauntingly in the shallow water, while the figures gazing toward the horizon give the setting an air of wistfulness. Ferrez used light in ways that enhanced the beauty of the landscape at the same time as he documented his subjects' utility.

Views like Ferrez's composition of Rio de Janeiro's Sugar Loaf Mountain stun the eye with its stylish combinations of geometric shapes and human figures contemplating nature (2.12). Ferrez attained a reputation for quality, but the public never made him a success, being unwilling to pay a photographer to do what they thought was the province of artists. His ability to capture engineering triumphs, like the

2.13 Ferrez, Ascending tram, GF

view of the motorized tram ascending Corcovado Mountain, remains the hallmark of his work (2.13).

Career paths in commercial photography diversified further as urban life became more complex and the marketplace expanded to support further specialization. A career more prolific and broad based than the usual was that of Militão Augusto de Azevedo (1837–1905). Starting as a street photographer in São Paulo in 1862, he eventually became a *carte de visite* portraitist, operating for some years a local affiliate of the prestigious *carioca* Carneiro and Gaspar Studio, until he opened his own establishment, "Photographic Americana."

Important to Militão's success was the drop in prices for photographic work, which enabled him to serve a clientele of relatively ordinary people.[36] Twelve thousand of his miniature portraits survive in the possession of his descendants. Militão photographed not only former slaves, professors, soldiers, clowns, priests, and other "representative types," but also many men, women, and children of the middle and upper classes. When he did photograph members of high society, in fact, his lower social status probably intimidated him.[37] His studio poses are unremarkable individually, following posing convention, but in the aggregate they provide a visual census of a generation of subjects.

The elaborate hairdo and billowing dress of the young society woman in 2.14a, barely beyond her teens, gives her the aspect of a matron as ornate as her furniture. Her wooden, sidewise posture adds to this impression. Azevedo's *carte* exudes haughtiness and social distance. In contrast, the show girl of 2.14b wears a skirt pulled up almost to her knees and faces the camera provocatively, looking directly at the viewer. Both her costume and her pose mark her as an immodest exotic, clearly of a lower social class. Her bodice is tight and revealing, in brisk contrast to the society matron's layered clothing, which hides her figure and dwarfs her face. Even the vantage point of the lens is instructive: the society belle is photographed straight on, the chorus girl from slightly below, adding a relaxed, sensual dimension because it shows her legs.

São Paulo was a slow-growing commercial city of less than 23,000 inhabitants in 1855.

2.14a Azevedo, *Carte de visite*, HH

2.14b Azevedo, *Carte de visite*, HH

Militão's street scenes show a city that was poor, empty, and gloomy; a visitor in 1861 called it "sad, monotonous, almost depressing."[38] The accepted social code prevented women of good standing from leaving their homes, so the city in his photographs seems devoid of women, except for domestics. His outdoor photographs over a period of twenty years document the growth of the city, which by the 1870s had begun to stir as a result of the expansion of coffee agriculture to the west and south of Rio de Janeiro. Subsidized immigration brought thousands of Italian peasants to the coffee fields; by 1900 as many as two-thirds of the region's population was Italian-born. Militão and others photographed the newcomers as curiosities but also as sought-after arrivals to the New World. The photographs of immigrant agriculturists which survive illustrate the photographers' respect.

Benjamin Franklin Pease was a Peruvian contemporary of Militão de Azevedo. He arrived in Lima in 1852 and purchased a studio run by another daguerreotypist, Arturo Terry. Pease married a Peruvian woman and thereby gained access to the elite. By 1856 he was established to the point where President Ramón Castilla sat for him. Pease used North American merchandising devices, notably advertising and publicity hype. He dealt with his chief competition, the studios of Amandus Moller, by importing two American photographers from New York (H. D. W. Moulton and V. L. Richardson) and announcing them "with hyperbolic fanfare."[39] Moller countered by hiring them away and baiting Pease in the press. In 1863, when four of the five largest photo studios in Lima agreed among themselves to fix prices (in order to combat declining profits caused by competition), Pease refused. The advertisement announcing the fee schedule claimed that the agreement would assure the maintenance of "the art of photography in the state of splendor and progress which it has attained in Lima," despite the fact that materials and chemical products were much more costly there than elsewhere, and that "it is indispensable that a moderate charge should not bring down that art to a vulgar level without merit."[40]

The history of Pease's business illustrates how daguerreotypists and portraitists working alone could aspire to own successful businesses. In early 1859 Pease moved out of his small studio to a grand salon in his building.[41] Pease stayed open evenings, to attract more clients, and sold paintings in addition to his photographic portraits. Given that few public places in any Latin American city were open to anyone without membership, the creation of the photographic galleries represented an enhancement of the quality of urban life. More typical, perhaps, of the career patterns of professional photographers in the nineteenth century was the case of Christiano Júnior (1830–1902), a *carte de visite* cameraman. His lucid photographs of blacks taken in Brazil in the period between 1864 and 1866 were sold in Rio de Janeiro as curiosities at the price of 28 *mil-réis* for ten sets, or ten times the monthly wage of a free laborer.[42] Christiano was one of the legions of itinerant photographers who wandered from one Latin American country to another. Likely a Portuguese immigrant to Brazil, he moved his base of operations from Brazil to Argentina in 1876 after a dozen or so years in Rio de Janeiro. He turned to selling hand-mounted travel albums of views of rural Argentina, winning a gold medal at the 1871 Cordoba Exposition and another at the

Scientific Exposition of Buenos Aires in 1876. Two years later he sold his studio in the Argentine capital, with an inventory of 25,000 glass plates, to an Englishman, A. S. Witcomb. He then moved to Paraguay where he attempted to support his retirement by hand painting portraits taken by other photographers in Asunción. His obituary noted that the old man, "once famous in *porteño* society," died impoverished and almost blind.[43]

When new photographic methods and trends penetrated Latin America, they did so unevenly and on a small scale. A four-lens *carte de visite* camera, which could record quadruple images simultaneously or in rapid succession, became commonplace in Europe by the mid-1860s but for the most part was not exported to Latin America. There, most photographers continued to work with single-image cameras, relying on their studio assistants to turn out the multiple copies from each exposure. Labor was cheap, compensating for the older and less efficient equipment. Itinerant photographers used assistants to deliver proofs to customers and take orders, while they moved on to the next town. Since the assistants also printed the orders, they

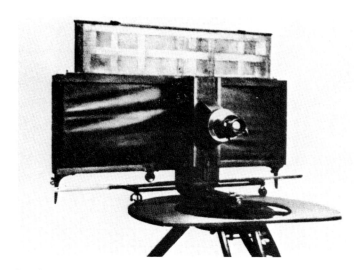

2.15 M. Brandon camera, GF

acquired the skills which permitted many of them to become photographers themselves. A few were blacks (in Brazil and Cuba) or Indians (in the Andean republics), although prestigious studios in the major cities were owned and operated by businessmen from elite racial groups or by European immigrants.[44] A broad range separated the most expensive work, for which clients were charged as much as sixty Peruvian pesos in 1860, from the cheapest *carte de visite* pasteboard, widely available for a single peso.[45] On the whole, though, photography served upper- and middle-class interests simultaneously. Both groups agreed exactly on which kinds of compositions best conveyed Latin American life: images depicting progress, sophistication, affluence, elegance—and the docility of the lower classes.

The subjects

In time photographers sharpened the ways in which they treated their subjects. Some cameramen employed unusual backgrounds. In 2.16, Brazil's Empress, draped in a dark, European dress with bustle, strikes a formal pose in front of a studio set framed by palms, rubber tree branches, and other tropical foliage.

Photographers in Europe, especially Disdéri in Paris, began to advocate capturing the "whole man," to create a kind of photographic theater of psychological expressiveness. Some fashionable Latin American photographers followed Disdéri's lead, but most anchored themselves in what by now had become compositional clichés. The English photographer, William Gaensly, created a series of portraits of Brazilian slaves, aiming to depict their exotic nature. In the portrait of a black man, photographed in Gaensly's studio, the subject's tribal scars, applied in Africa, show clearly (2.17).

Photographers continued to record street people and "types," selling most of the portraits as curiosities and souvenirs. Many of the subjects were poor, yet the scenes capturing their livelihoods wholly lacked social commentary.

Collectors prized images that tickled their imaginations—exotic tribesmen, remote natural wonders, humble slaves, risqué women—all to be enjoyed in the controlled and morally safe atmosphere of the home. The subjects of most of these portraits posed passively, confirming their uncomplaining role in the social order. A rare snapshot of a slave woman emptying water from a heavy vessel into a jar on the floor, captures the burden of domestic work which extended, with little respite, throughout the day (2.18).

Passivity of pose reflected the generalized apathy and enforced difference which characterized the Latin American lower classes well into the nineteenth century. These people probably had little choice: brutal treatment by police and harsh labor practices, combined with a social system hostile to upward mobility, especially for nonwhites, set the tone for their lives.

Consider the striking uniformity in the way Marc Ferrez posed vendors in the streets of Rio de Janeiro—always in front of a large canvas backdrop (2.19–2.23; visible in 2.19). His primary purpose seems to have been to illustrate these people's livelihood: selling newspapers,

2.16 Empress Teresa Cristina, GF

sharpening scissors, selling unusual food. The men and boys pictured here vary in race, age, physiognomy, and mein, but Ferrez ignores those differences; rather, each subject is subsumed by the composition and by its theme.

We can only guess at how people reacted when confronted by the intimidating presence of photographer and apparatus.[46] Some lower-class men and women stared at the camera listlessly; others appear to be carefree. Whites, who usually were European immigrants, and blacks, likely slaves or ex-slaves, showed similar degrees of weariness, but whites usually wore shoes and were better dressed. Shoelessness remained a mark of the black and the Indian in Latin American society long into the twentieth century.

The best subjects learned to hide their self-consciousness. In the early days of photography many people—even those from the educated classes—were apprehensive of being "robbed" by the alchemy of the photographic process. Balzac likened his sitting for the eminent portraitist, Gaspard Félix Nadar, to having his pocket picked. Less sophisticated men and women feared that their photographic images

2.17 Gaensly, Portrait of a black man, ca. 1880, GF

2.18 Goston, Slave woman, GF

2.19 Ferrez, Vendor "types," GF

2.20 Ferrez, Vendor "types," GF

2.21 Ferrez, Vendor "types," GF

2.22 Ferrez, Vendor "types," GF

2.23 Ferrez, Vendor "types," GF

2.24 Frond, "La Cuisine," GF

were double selves, and that harm would come to them if something were to happen at any subsequent time to the paper image. But the forces of social intimidation outweighed private terrors; the poor stood before the camera lens, specimens for their audiences.[47]

Victor Frond posed four black women in a frozen tableau, gave his image the Frenchified Portuguese title "La Cuisine à la Roça ("Rustic Meal"), and produced it as a lithograph (2.24). The spindly vegetation lends harshness to the scene, which is further accentuated by the unhappy air of the women, their clothing, and their primitive implements. The composition bears a striking resemblance to the products of the naturalist school of drawing employed by artists traveling with foreign scientific expeditions into the mid-nineteenth century. Since photographs were cheaper, photographers soon rendered these artists obsolete, absorbing, with little change, their way of presenting subjects.

Some of the subjects taken from the common people stood proudly, having joined the fantasy world created by the photographer on exactly the same basis as the Colombian merchant posing as a Frenchman or the Chilean "family of the better class" showing off their European finery. *Cartes de visite* were socially acceptable. The stiff, unadorned cardboard held benefits for the less affluent as well; they were rugged and they could be nailed to the wall. By 1860 there were as many as a dozen photographic studios in every main Latin American city, or one for every 10,000 inhabitants. In 1862 a newspaper article in Lima's *El Comercio* chided the popular practice of exchanging photos, claiming that the average family had to spend the equivalent of thirty dollars a year on such frivolities.

Carte photographers specialized in "types" of the romanticized past. Indians provided popular subjects. This was part of the *costumbrista* tradition of depicting in precise detail the figures of aboriginal culture, and also part of the mid-nineteenth-century penchant for attributing noble and spiritual characteristics to Indians, especially the long-gone Incas (and in Brazil the fictional Iracema and the single-breasted Amazons). An English visitor to Peru in 1873 likened the visages of the models for the *carte de visite* series, "The Incas of Peru," to the English vignettes of the ancient English kings in English history books. "Take off their big ears . . .

dock off a feather or two here and there, and you have the Anglo-Saxon monarchs of our school-boy duty . . . for the Incas."[48] The subjects themselves were secondary. Three Indians are posed dramatically in 2.25, forming a triangle which confronts the camera. But their faces are set into a kind of grimness; they sit silently uncooperative.

The affluent classes formed the core of every photographer's business; they were portrayed to show off their elegance and social importance. Whole families were marched off to sit for portraits. Often nursemaids held their charges in their arms, the child always the focal point of the image. In 2.26a a child dressed in white literally sits on a pedestal; his black Brazilian slave nursemaid crouches, presumably to remain as unobtrusive as possible. In another picture a Peruvian child is held at the center of the composition by a domestic servant who seems not to be making eye contact with the lens, and whose face is almost entirely obscured by shadow (2.26b).

Photographers recorded public works ceremonies, political banquets, civic festivals, the opening of the racing season—in short, the

2.25 Courret, Indians, HH

public lives of the men and women of the gentry. Augusto Malta carefully posed the dignitaries at the inauguration of Rio de Janeiro's elevated Central Railroad line in 1907 (2.27). The Brazilian president is there, accompanied by his three elegantly coiffed women, an army general, engineers, and officials, all posturing for posterity.

Latin American documentary photography
By the mid-1860s photography had taken its place in urban centers around the world as a dynamic cultural expression linked in the public mind to technological and industrial progress. There was still some overlap with paintings and drawings by naturalist artists (as late as 1887 the pictorialist Rodolfo Amando Philippi sold hand-drawn scenes of rural life in Chile using virtually the same compositional genre as the newly emerged photodocumentarists), but photography increasingly supplanted the work of artists.[49]

Photographs documented new social realities as technology facilitated the shift of population from rural to urban areas, the proliferation of fast trains and ships, and accelerating economic

2.26a Anonymous, Nursemaid with child, UNM

2.26b Courret, Indian servant and Peruvian child, HH

growth. Railroads and accompanying engineering feats of the mid-nineteenth century altered perceptions of geography and space, threatening the old sense of order; but photographs, increasingly accessible to the public, helped shape and solidify these perceptions. The disorienting effects of material change were, in a sense, subdued by the new medium, which made these changes concrete.[50]

Foreign photographers, both freelance and on contract, continued to come to Latin America seeking images that would appeal to collectors. The pasteboards of the 1860s yielded in popularity, in the following decade, to the stereoscopic camera, which created the illusion of three dimensions. It took the public by storm. Oliver Wendell Holmes in 1859 called it "the card of introduction to make all mankind acquaintances."[51] For several decades stereographic cards brought the world to the parlors of the well-to-do.[52] The results were significant. Foreign commercial firms sent a new battery of photographers to the region, and local photographers found new outlets for sales.

Stereoscope viewers, sometimes called stereopticons, sold for sixty-two cents in the United

2.27 Inauguration of Rio de Janeiro's elevated railroad, HH

States in 1860 and as little as twenty-four cents by the turn of the century, when the market was dominated by Sears, Roebuck and other large firms. A hand unit and sixty views of the San Francisco earthquake were available for less than a dollar within months of the tragedy. Dozens of companies sent photographers to Latin America and the Caribbean and sold thousands of sets of stereoscope view cards on Latin American subjects; two major firms were Underwood and Underwood (founded in 1882) and the Keystone View Company (founded in 1888). Stereoscope sales climbed steadily until they levelled off in the early 1920s, when competition from new leisure activities, especially mass-circulation magazines, reduced the popularity of the medium (see 2.28).

We do not know to what extent Latin American elites collected stereoscope views of their own countries, but they probably acquired view cards of foreign countries just as their counterparts did elsewhere. The creation of a worldwide audience for images of foreign places, in any case, hardened the divisions between studio photography in Latin American cities, which continued to take photographs of elite men,

women and children and, in time, record their ceremonial occasions (christenings, communions, infant deaths, weddings, milestone festivities), and the freelance stereoscopic photographers.

The advent of the stereoscopic camera reinforced the tendency to shoot urban curiosities (street eccentrics, slaves, children, artisans, and especially indigenous people in native dress), standard architectural views, and the always popular exotic images of primitive peoples in remote locales. If any distinction between the output of local and foreign contract photographers could be seen, it was that the former, who often were hired by banks, utility companies, and government agencies, maintained the earlier-established photographic tradition emphasizing technical and material progress, whereas the latter tended to look for the unusual and the exotic, although always presenting them in safe, visually controlled ways.

Documentary photography had arrived in Latin America, widening the gap between the local studio photographers, who were wedded to the *carte* trade and family portraiture, and the foreign contract photographers, who

sought scenes to be reproduced and viewed in stereopticons. The first documentarists produced panoramic vistas of cities, photographing the waterfront in coastal locations or highlighting urban growth in mountainous inland cities. Using large-format cameras, they often created horizontal montages in which three, four, or more exposures were displayed side by side, presenting a view of 180 degrees or more. Marc Ferrez invented a giant camera which produced an angle of vision so broad that one exposure could take in an entire cityscape.[53]

Two of the best documentarists were Benito Panunzi and a German named Heffer. Panunzi roamed Buenos Aires province during the decade of the 1860s. (He disappeared thereafter, his fate unknown.) Panunzi recorded architectural scenes and presented gaucho life in relatively unadorned fashion, contrary to Argentine myth that idealized the cowboy of the plains as a folk hero. Heffer worked mostly in Chile, producing panoramic views of nature. His photographs of the snow-capped Andes were especially popular among his collector clients. In his scene of Mt. Cervin in Chile's Valley of Desolation (2.29) Heffer poses a man

2.28 Stereographic card, Cuban family, RF

2.29 Heffer, "Valley of Desolation," Chile, ca. 1880, HH

wrapped in a wool poncho not only to lend scale to the scene but to remind viewers of man's civilizing presence in the Latin American wilderness.[54]

By recording physical and architectural progress, photographers helped to claim legitimacy for incumbent regimes publicly committed to progress. They served governments in other ways as well. Eleven years after James Robertson and Roger Fenton shocked the British public (1855) with scenes from the Crimean War, an Uruguayan photographer named M. Baté recorded hundreds of scenes from the Paraguayan War, including grisly images of piles of soldiers' bodies rotting in the sun.[55] The Argentine general Júlio A. Roca engaged three official photographers to accompany his six thousand troops on his "Conquest of the Desert" in 1879, an expedition which wiped out most of the remaining "savage" indigenous tribes of the pampa and whose brutal military success made Roca a national hero and gained him the presidency.

An Italian-born Argentine, Antonio Pozzo, worked as a publicist for the positivist "Generation of 80," especially for *caudillo*

Adolfo Alsina (he even named his studio "Fotografia Alsina"). Most of Pozzo's photographs taken during Roca's expedition glorified it, although some of his shots of Indian *caciques* and their families, "pacified" by military action, are a poignant reminder of the tragedy of the campaign. For his services as military photographer, Pozzo received the rank of captain, some decorations, and a piece of land.

The documentarists—from Panunzi and Stahl in the 1860s to their counterparts well into the early decades of the twentieth century —represented the best in technical quality and imagination in Latin American photographic history. Although they followed naturalist convention, seeking literal representation of their subjects, the most skillful among them managed to produce haunting images that were brought to life by their visual strength. The careers of the Latin American documentarists essentially paralleled the Grand Style photographers, which documented the ascendancy of North American cities, and which ranked as the most complete public expression of the American urban renaissance at the World's Columbian Exposition, held in Chicago in 1892.[56] But

Latin American view photography did fall behind, lacking the opportunities for recognition and profit made possible by mass merchandising in North America and the willingness of civic officials there to pay for varied photographic services. Latin American photographers continued to be reminded that buyers were staid and conservative in their preferences. Even when invited to exhibitions they were constrained by prevailing notions of propriety. At the 1875 Chilean International Exposition in Santiago, the local photographers' entries were predictably celebratory.[57] No market opportunity in Latin America equaled that of photography for disseminating propaganda or portraying sensational events. But when photographs of disasters or other compelling events were published in illustrated magazines in Latin America, captions rarely identified the photographer by name.[58]

Latin American photographers did lend their skills for political ends. Political parties bought photomontage portraits of their leaders and used *carte*-sized photographs to hand out for publicity purposes. Opposition groups used trick images to caricature or ridicule. The

Peruvian studio photographer Villroy L. Richardson, a supporter of reformist presidential aspirant Manuel Pardo, was imprisoned for his photomontage caricatures during the 1872 campaign. His grisly photograph of two victims (the Gutierrez brothers) lynched by a mob after a failed military coup, purportedly depicted the naked bodies hanging from the towers of Lima's Cathedral before throngs of bystanders— "witness," in the words of the United States legation chief, "of the popular power."[59] Photographic caricatures used for political purposes appeared frequently in most Latin American countries by the last third of the nineteenth century, although none as graphic as the Richardson photograph, which recent research has definitively shown to be doctored.[60]

The more that improved technology facilitated departures from established photographic convention, the more European and North American photographers perfected new forms of expression. In contrast, the visual diversity of Latin American photography evolved slowly. British and European photographers rushed to the countryside to capture on film the vanishing life of the rural seaside. In the United States rapid demographic expansion provoked cultural dislocations, threatening the bonding mechanisms behind popular culture (myths, folktales, ways of communicating) that had linked urban life to rural outposts; photographers helped build a new psychological synthesis, as comforting as it seemed authoritative.[61]

In the United States (and to some degree across the Atlantic) the stage was now set for the rise of socially conscious documentary photography, although the majority of view photographers continued to earn their living from corporate or civic sponsors, which dampened their opportunities for photographic editorializing. In Latin America, if photographers had a heightened awareness of the brutality of social existence, it was not obvious in their output. Prevailing positivist values adopted the laissez-faire ideals of the Enlightenment, and were seen not as tools to bring freedom to the masses but to protect the status quo.

Latin America, in the second half of the nineteenth century, witnessed material progress, mostly in urbanization and accompanying export-oriented infrastructure (railroads, improvements in communications, municipal improvements, port facilities). As the quality of life improved for the elites, it deteriorated in many ways for the average citizen. Opportunities for upward mobility were limited. Dissent and political criticism were not tolerated; political change, when it did occur, almost never represented a sharp break with the past.[62] Fear of latent social instability and the passionate desire among the ruling elites to preserve nominal unity in values—borrowing foreign ideas but stripping them of any potentially egalitarian content—yielded an environment which stifled creativity. This was seen in everything from culture, which contained many derivative elements, to business practices, which relied on serving elite interests, ignoring the potentially large internal mass market. Photographers, as well as writers, artists, architects, and anyone else who might have benefitted from an atmosphere favoring experimentation in forms of expression, faced powerful constraints on the directions their careers could take.

North American prosperity, despite the depression of the 1890s, created a market for photographic images almost as large as the population itself. Portrait studios still turned out stylized photographs of family members decked out in elegant clothing (often requested by poor immigrant clients anxious to send home photographs showing them at their best). Other photographers made their living in the new field of advertising, or working for publicity firms, or as photographers of nature. An entire branch of photography produced images for use in education and publishing. Meanwhile, in Latin America, still plagued by political instability and paying the price of decades of neo-colonial dependence, photographic opportunities only improved incrementally from the first years when photography was still a popular novelty among the upper classes. The divergence between Latin American photography and its North American and European counterparts was sharpest between 1885 and 1895, when, from Mexico to Patagonia, photography was essentially a compiler of facts—an auxiliary service to enterprises seeking to record the facade of order and progress enforced by strong measures of social control and the suppression of remnants of African, and especially indigenous, cultures.

Traditional documentary photography gave

way in the United States and Europe in the mid-1890s to a revisionist school whose photographers now used their cameras to destroy the image of the progressive city they had helped to create, to expose the ills of city life in a crusade for social reform. They were aided by technological innovations, such as lighter cameras and artificial light, which allowed them to photograph dark corners of city streets and even the interiors of factories, tenements, and jails. Jacob A. Riis and Lewis Hine in the United States, and John Thompson of the Royal Geographic Society in London, electrified their audiences with views of slum life and the evils of industrial society, as did Brassai, Henri Cartier-Bresson, and others later on the continent.[63]

In Latin America, photographers remained recorders of community achievement; and they remained businessmen, pure and simple. But some major changes in social mores were brought about by the photographic revolution itself. Through the mid-1860s portraits of young women of socially prominent families were considered as sacred as their persons, and it was considered scandalous if these images were to fall into licentious hands. Photogra-

phers offered to destroy plates after printing; and they traveled to the homes of their clients, which was more discreet than photographing in the studio. Some women from the upper class covered their faces with dark veils, affecting a Moorish custom, and wore special garments, the *saya y manto*, which covered them to their ankles.[64] But by the 1870s and 1880s photographic portraits had become so accepted that, as Keith McElroy showed, "it became a mark of flattery to have portraits of beauties from prominent families sold commercially."[65]

The great increase in amateur photography by the 1880s significantly narrowed business opportunities for professional photographers in Latin America. In 1884 there were at least one thousand amateurs in Havana alone.[66] George Eastman transformed photography around the world in 1888 with his Kodak No. 1 camera. The box camera produced a "vast tide" of unpretentious images which were satisfactory to most. Unwittingly, snapshots revolutionized the ways in which people saw, since amateur photographs did not follow compositional convention but were filled with things more or less accidentally framed by the lens.[67]

Studio photographers survived by retreating even further into the bourgeois fantasy of gentility, preciousness, and safety, and by using their technical mastery to produce stylized images beyond the amateurs' reach.[68] When they ventured outdoors they invariably composed their subjects according to idealized visions of a conflict-free society. Photographic expression ossified; humor, when it appeared, was self-conscious or ironic. Rather than broaden its perspective and potential social utility, professional photography retreated into a private world of dated, predictable imagery.

Two new visual forms that became immensely popular at the turn of the century provided opportunities for commercial photographers in the same stultifying mode. One was the photographic postcard. It usually depicted civic landmarks or panoramic views of large areas of cities, invariably stressing the typical rather than the particular; as a result it provided few opportunities for photographic creativity.[69] Millions circulated: in 1909 fifteen million were mailed in Brazil, a country of twenty million people.[70] Postcards attained comparable levels of use in practically every Latin American country. Virtually every photographer produced postcards or sold views to postcard manufacturers. The postcards simply repeated the old conventions: famous scenes, "typical" people, hackneyed poses.

The same was true for the second new vehicle, the photographic "Blue Book," or publicity yearbook. First produced by foreign firms (Philadelphia, New Orleans, Brussels, Paris) and later manufactured locally, they were subsidized by local or national governments or private firms, and usually distributed gratis as a form of advertising. They were shamelessly boosterish, using stylized photographs of officials, composite photographs of *Flores* (society dames: "combinación de Belleza é Intelectualidad"), and shots of military officers, prize-winning animals, public works, buildings, parks, harvest-laden fields, and produce-laden trains and docks. They were often printed bilingually, for foreign distribution or display at international expositions. Virtually every nation, state, municipality, public utility, and thousands of banks, schools, social clubs, and commercial associations subsidized these testimonies to progress.[71] Thousands of photographic collages were distributed during electoral campaigns at all levels of political contest (2.30a and b).

Economic and technological change did provide some new opportunities for more creative photographic specialization. Travel became easier and the first illustrated magazines appeared, supplementing traditional opportunities for sale of documentary-style photographs.[72] Combat photographers accompanied newspaper journalists to various conflicts, including the War of the Pacific, the Paraguayan War, the Canudos uprising in Brazil, and the secession of Panama from Colombia, although they remained at some distance from actual fighting.[73] An Argentine-based Spanish lensman, Juan Gutiérrez, died in action in the Bahian backlands in 1897. Interest widened for visual records of contemporary events.

In Mexico the tradition of documentary photography was nurtured under the positivist dictatorship of Porfírio Díaz, and achieved its fullest maturity during the Revolution in the work of Agustín Víctor Casasola. Under Díaz photojournalism served the dictatorship, emphasizing public works construction, diplomatic pomp, parades, and posed photographs of orderly citizens, all in the Latin American positivist tradition.[74] Traveling with the Villista troops

and focusing his attention on life among the ordinary soldiers, Casasola's lens captured memorable glimpses of the human side of the conflict, especially photographs of Indian women accompanying their men, and of women fighters. Casasola saw himself as a chronicler of the war in the Matthew Brady tradition. His photographs of Emiliano Zapata (alive and after his assassination) and Pancho Villa commanding his troops, and his many shots of executions and the carnage of war, number among the most frequently remembered documentary images of Latin American historical events (2.31).[75]

To some degree Casasola represented an intermediate approach between the traditional attitude of documentary photographers, that "the act of recording takes precedence over the act of interpreting,"[76] and that of the activist or reformist photojournalists, typified by Jacob Riis. Like Riis, Casasola often wrote texts to accompany his images, and he personally supported the Revolution. His archives, which are located in Mexico City, contain more than 400,000 negatives from a career spanning the closing years of the Díaz regime through the Cárdenas

2.31 Casasola, *Soldier and family,* AM

administration's revival of the Revolution's agenda in 1938. Casasola's images were dramatic —"history posturing for the lens," in the words of Mexican historian Carlos Monsivais. Essentially a journalist, his documentary tradition later influenced the art-photography movement (personified by Manuel Alvarez Bravo), which was rooted in the search for a distinctive Latin American cultural identity.[77]

Another photographer working in Mexico, the German-born Hugo Brehme, captured similarly stark images of the Revolution, including a train-top encampment of Villista soldiers and their families pathetically huddled with all of their possessions.[78] A Uruguayan, Jesús Cubela, photographed similar images of troops in his country in the 1880s, as did such Cuban lensmen as Francisco López Rubio and Emilio Prado during the pre-Independence conflicts of the 1890s, and Brazilian war photographers during the campaign against the Canudos uprising in Bahia in 1897.

Social and technological changes ushered in after World War I further limited career choices for photographers in Latin America. By 1914 the building industry abandoned revival style in favor of new forms based on geometric patterns. The budding modernist movement directed attention away from nostalgic images of the past to new forms of experimentation. But virtually none of the outlets for photographic experimentation that opened up elsewhere were present in Latin America. North American and European photographers like Alfred Stieglitz, who used the camera to scrutinize urban life—not necessarily to reform it, but to inspect its nuances—simply had no counterparts in Latin America.[79] Only a handful of photographers were able to survive economically and still inject a sense of vision into their work. Interestingly, two of the most notable exceptions, Martín Chambi and Sebastian Rodriguez, were Indians from the high Andes. Using battered, old-fashioned cameras and subsisting as village studio photographers in the traditional mode, they managed to capture life in probing, sometimes brilliant fashion. The marketplace being what it was, they survived, but neither became affluent nor particularly acclaimed. To be sure, their lower-class origins and second-class status colored the ways they posed their clients. But it was the uncanny eye

of both of these men, their ability to see into the personalities of their subjects, that lent magic to their photographs. Scores of other Andean natives worked as photographers in the region over the decades, but their output was as conventional as the work of middle-class photographers from the big cities.

Peruvian Martín Chambi, who worked for four decades beginning in the early 1920s, produced thousands of photographs in the documentary mode despite the severe limitations imposed by the necessity to earn a living in the remote city of Cuzco. The son of *campesinos* from the village of Coaza, Chambi apprenticed with a photographer working for a British mining company and finally settled in Cuzco. He earned a modest living as a studio and commercial photographer, although he traveled widely in the region, influenced by the rise of *indigenista* consciousness in Peru in the early 1920s. Cuzco was a center for pro-Indianist sentiment among artisans and intellectuals, and many of his friends were probably members of the Peruvian Communist Party, which was founded in Cuzco. He became a close friend of José Uriel García, author of the Indianist *El*

Nuevo Indio. Chambi associated with the Aprista party after its establishment in 1924 on a nationalistic and pro-Indian platform.

Chambi's photographic genius was his capacity to extract from everyday scenes ways of portraying his subjects that brought them to life without alienating convention (for he was subject to the extremely conservative rules of Peruvian society). He apparently posed his photographs so meticulously that he was able to satisfy his upper-class clients without them perceiving that he was satirizing their gravity and display of status and class-derived power.[80] Consider his 1928 outdoor portrait of the Cesar Lomellini family in Cuzco (2.32a). There is smugness here, perhaps a touch of superiority. The man in sunglasses and cap lounges too comfortably for a photograph with his father and mother; the young man in riding boots grins too much. The grandchildren are dressed in shimmering white, contrasting with the dark and formal attire of their elders. Posing the group on rocks and hillocks adds incongruity to the scene.

Chambi's portrait of his own family lacks affectation of any kind (2.32b). Chambi himself

2.32a Chambi, Lomellini family, MC

2.32b Chambi, Chambi family, MC

2.33 Chambi, Wedding portrait, MC

sits as the traditional head of a family would,
but his wife and children appear natural,
though stiff. Were even Chambi's family members intimidated by the lens and its symbol-
ism of upper-class life? The children wear light-
colored clothing, but not angelic white.

Consider his 1926 photograph captioned
"Wedding Couple, Cuzco" (2.33) If they are
man and wife, the distance between the two in
age and manner seems striking. The girl appears childlike, the man tired, stiff, distant. If he
is the bride's father, the distance remains. There
is no affection between the two; they stare
into space as if resigned to a life without
happiness.[81] Chambi was somehow able to go
so much further than other photographers in
penetrating the social realities of his day. Un-
fortunately, most of his work remained in the
Cuzco region, and he died in 1973 largely
unknown.

Most documentary photographers were less
successful in winning the trust of their subjects.
In the Mexican pilgrimage scene a woman
makes her way, on her knees, up the Monte
Sacro, a distance of nearly four kilometers to
the shrine (2.34). Her face is contorted, and she

2.34 Waite, "Doing penance," UNM

2.35 Rodriguez, Peasants celebrating Carnival, FA

is supported by onlookers. Is what shows in their faces attributable to the nature of the event, or to the intrusion of the camera?

At least one other Chambi contemporary produced beautiful and eloquent images, capturing in similar ways the texture of local life without distancing himself from his subjects: Sebastian Rodriguez, born in Huancayo in 1896 to a tailor's family, and one of seven children. Like Chambi he started as an apprentice to an established studio photographer before setting up a studio in the Morococha, a bleak mining town in the Central Highlands established in 1902 by the Cerro de Pasco Corporation. Mine workers, mostly Indian peasants and some literate mestizos, like Rodriguez, came to Morococha from neighboring locales, especially from the Mantaro Valley. Rodriguez used a battered Agfa camera and glass plates to photograph them. Both Chambi and Rodriguez belonged to a vernacular photographic culture, practiced under severe economic limitations by utilitarian photographers who came out of the same social world as their subjects. Only recently have these photographers and their work been recognized as valid (and exciting) subjects for study.[82]

Rodriguez's photographs symbolically linked the mining camp to the villages where the miners' families lived.[83] He movingly documented their lives: the constant specter of mine collapse and death, the transformation of Indian peasants into professional miners, labor violence, and the activities of the families.[84] In a photograph captioned "Peasants Celebrating Carnavales in Morococha," the photographer captured the mining town's merging of two cultures (2.35). The women wear traditional Indian dress, the men miner's garb. The frail artifacts of gaiety—paper streamers around the celebrants—contrast bitterly with the air of bleakness and ragged poverty, especially vivid in the tattered clothing of the young boy and the ill-fitting shoes of the two children in the lower portion of the photograph.

A second photograph, circa 1928, shows the funeral of a miner killed in an accident (2.36). The background, overlooking a valley, is remorselessly lifeless. The posed mourners, carrying candles, circle the dead man, who will be buried in a polished wooden coffin which seems to have more material substance than anything else in the photograph.

The Rodriguez photograph in 2.37 would be harsh enough without its awful caption, "Rapist and Victim in the Stockade." The grizzled prisoner and the tiny, preadolescent girl stand framed by smartly dressed law officers. Observe the feet of the four figures: the polished military boots, the rapist's worn shoes pointing outward, the girl's innocent open stance below her hat held modestly in front of her skirt. The grinning figure behind the stockade fence lends an air of mockery to the framed scene.

As we have seen, the slow development of local markets for visual images, combined with the elite's preference for imitating foreign culture, severely limited creative opportunities for professional photographers in Latin America. But those photographers who managed to maintain high esthetic standards (as well as make a living) produced images equal to those anywhere in the world. Even though they usually worked for municipal authorities and other local clients with positive image-building in mind, the daguerreotype masters of the 1840s managed to elevate their work from the static separation of bodies from space characteristic of

2.36 Rodriguez, Miner's funeral, FA

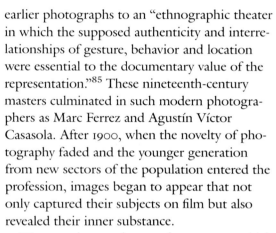

earlier photographs to an "ethnographic theater in which the supposed authenticity and interrelationships of gesture, behavior and location were essential to the documentary value of the representation."[85] These nineteenth-century masters culminated in such modern photographers as Marc Ferrez and Agustín Víctor Casasola. After 1900, when the novelty of photography faded and the younger generation from new sectors of the population entered the profession, images began to appear that not only captured their subjects on film but also revealed their inner substance.

We can only speculate on the extent to which Martín Chambi, Sebastian Rodriguez, and perhaps other itinerant photographers consciously produced images with meaning beyond their commercial purpose. Reading photographs, after all, is a subjective, interpretive act that relies as much on the viewer, the corporeal state of the image itself, and the technical processes by which the image was produced as on the intent of the photographer or the physical appearance of his subject. This endeavor, to interpret the images produced by Latin America's photographers, is the central aim of the following chapters.

Part Two   Photographs as Evidence

Evidence is not usually accepted with closed eyes.
Benedetto Croce, History

I T WOULD be as imprudent to offer hard-and-fast rules for "reading" visual documents as it is for reading written historical sources. Images are capable of many, many interpretations. But some guidelines can be offered, especially if we see photographs as pieces in a larger puzzle, not as facts in themselves. Preserved visual images complement the historian's effort to reconstruct the past. They illuminate special qualities inherent in the subject or in the mind of the photographer, or in the relationship between the two.

This chapter outlines an approach to the historical analysis of photographs. In explaining this approach to "reading photographs," ten general themes are applied to a collection of Latin American images—all historical documents in one sense or another. Each of the themes is elaborated by specific questions, which are designed to transport the viewer into the photograph. Some of these questions overlap, others stand alone, valuable for one kind of scrutiny, less useful for others. The ten themes are: (1) photographs as evidence, (2) the photographer's intention, (3) society's values and norms, (4) probing unstated norms, (5) depiction of social relationships, (6) everyday life, (7) unexpected or suppressed information, (8) romanticization, (9) satire and irony, and (10) change over time.

1. Photographs as evidence

How do standard historians' questions about written documents apply to visual images? Issues of attribution—time, place, bias, intentions, audience—apply to photographs as well as to written sources. What were the (author's) photographer's intentions and interests at the moment of (writing) exposure? For whom was the visual image composed and reproduced? What purpose did it serve? How much in the evidence is new, how much deliberate, how much repetitive, how much the expression of unconscious desires and fears?[1]

We rarely know the specific date of nineteenth- and early twentieth-century photographs. Approximations can be made from evidence supplied by the plates themselves: the wet collodion process predominated until about 1880, when processes using larger dry plates replaced it. In some cases, such as the work of Marc Ferrez, we know that all surviving glass plates date from after 1873, when a fire destroyed his studio in Rio de Janeiro.[2] But since most available archival photographs are attributed either anonymously or to studios no longer in existence, we frequently have nothing to go on but the print itself.

It is helpful to learn as much as possible about the historical context of a photograph, but old photographs usually carry few, if any, notations. Unless they were published during the photographer's lifetime, captions are likely missing or inaccurate. Photographs of famous people and historical events are easy enough to identify, but it is usually the more anonymous images of ordinary subjects which promise to shed light on society. Often entire collections of photographs stored in archives are simply filed under the collector's name or by generic title ("Mexico: Revolution," or "Cuba: City Life") with no additional information preserved. This is true in the United States as well as in Latin America.

Commentators on historical method press researchers to merge facts with ideas, which are contextual explanations based on facts but which lead to more significant conclusions.[3] Just as the discovery of a previously unknown letter, report, or other written document containing unexpected information can set the researcher on a totally new path of investigation, so a photograph can perform the same function.

The photograph of the official Pernambuco state delegation to the first national sugar growers' meeting in Brazil in 1902 (3.1) contains visual information about membership in the regional elite, which is unexplained in the extensive historical literature.[4] The photograph, captioned "Pernambucan Representatives to the First Sugar Conference," is subcaptioned "the sugar growing elite."[5] The names of all but five of the nineteen men are provided, confirming in verifiable terms that these men actually were the most prestigious members of the state's social and economic elite. The older men are grouped at the center, although all of the representatives who are identified shared the same degree of importance.

3.1 Sugar planters, IJN

The startling and unexpected "fact" in this photograph, totally absent from the written record, is the single black man in the upper row. Dressed exactly the same way as the others, he is identified as "Fulano Macedo França," in English, "First name unknown" Macedo França. That his family clan is identified but his own name not known adds to the mystery. The presence of a black in an official photograph of the highest echelon of the state elite, barely twenty years after the abolition of slavery in Brazil, suggests clearly that the elite did open its doors at least in one case. This is the fact conveyed by the photograph: it is so inexplicable that it demands rethinking of conventional explanations about its subject.

Does the publication in which a photograph was published offer information about how contemporaries saw the image? The photograph of Colombian child soldiers, two of them carrying rifles, appeared in a Parisian magazine, *L'illustration*, near the end of the War of a Thousand Days (1899–1902); the photographer is unattributed (3.2). One can surmise that the photographer was a foreign visitor, shocked by the presence of children in military service. By posing the boys

3.3 People on sidewalk in Salvador, Bahia, GF

centrally ringed by the bemused older soldiers, he is telling his viewers that this kind of practice was common in Latin America even if it was unnatural by their own standards. French readers of the publication were presumably shocked, Colombians not. The image of the ground was obviously retouched, highlighting the boy's uniforms, especially their feet, which were clad in canvas shoes, showing them to be of peasant origin.[6]

Is the image representative or anachronistic? Readers of historical description must always decode the words of the author and derive their own visual images. Recalling Richard Henry Dana Junior's precise and eloquent paragraphs describing the California coast, a wise historian warned that we must remember that Dana saw Santa Barbara and San Francisco bays after a voyage of 150 days and during a sunny interlude in the gloomy storm season.[7] Visual images should prompt a basic question: is the depiction typical?

A variant of this question asks whether portrayed behavior is natural or contrived. Photographic theorists speak about "political import" of photos: "confirmation and reduplication of subject-positions for the dominant discursive formations."[8] Jargon aside, what are people doing? Does their behavior seem believable? A good indication of the verisimilitude of a scene is the degree to which the subjects seem comfortable in (or estranged from) their environment.

Photo 3.3 depicts a fashionably dressed group of blacks on a sidewalk in Salvador, Bahia, in the early 1900s. The scene radiates urbanity. The tall man on the left wears a natty straw hat, a suit, and shined leather shoes, as does the man on the right walking toward the electrified trolley car. The two women, possibly mother and daughter, are dressed in sparkling white. We know nothing about the photographer or the circumstances during which the image was recorded. The scene suggests the existence of an affluent sector of the black population in a city which, although heavily Afro-Brazilian, was dominated by a light-skinned elite originating in the landed aristocracy. It is possible that the photograph represents normal street life, but given Brazil's racial map at the time it is highly unlikely. The scene was anomalous, if not

staged, and probably selected for its dramatic effect.[9]

A second example from Bahia raises the same caveat (3.4). This handsome portrait of a black man in formal dress and draped with a lavish emblematic sash suggests dignity, stature, achievement, and importance. It is the portrait of a physician attached to the prestigious Bahian Faculty of Medicine in the first decade of the twentieth century; it is the only black among more than seventy identical portraits stored in the archive of the Historical and Geographical Association of Salvador. Taken by itself it might well suggest fluid social mobility for blacks in the Bahia elite. But taken as a one-in-seventy circumstance, it offers a more subtle illustration of how limited were the exceptions to the rule. Like all documents, then, photographs must not be cited out of context.

3.4 Physician, Bahian Faculty of Medicine, IHB

Is there corroborative evidence beyond the visual image? Latin American society distinguished meaningfully between members of its own social aristocracy and foreigners; the latter often accumulated great wealth and power but rarely gained equivalent social and political acceptance.[10] In terms of dress and life-style, however, they were nearly indistinguishable, especially when posed in front of standardized studio backdrops. This is a case where visual evidence alone provides insufficient information: we must know more about family to be able to determine an individual or family's place in society. Studios favored generic captions for prints to sell to foreigners. Two examples of this are: "Home Life in the Family of a Cultivated and Wealthy Spanish Citizen," from Guayaquil at the turn of the century, and "Interior View of a Spanish Residence" from Mexico during the regime of Porfirio Díaz (3.5a and 3.5b). The captions imply that either the traveling photographer couldn't tell the difference between Latin Americans and Spaniards, or that the families had emigrated (unlikely), or that the subjects wanted to be considered Spaniards to enhance their prestige.[11]

3.5a "Spanish family," Ecuador, HH

3.5b "Spanish family," Mexico, HH

3.6 Mollendo, Bolivian port, 1880, HH

Do accompanying captions offer insight beyond the content of the image? A photographer named Mollendo in 1880 captured a haunting view of the Pacific coast: a passing freighter is partially obscured by the spray from waves breaking along the rocky shore (3.6). The caption, "Bolivians' Port to Ocean," places the photograph in context. At the battle of Tacna, early in 1880, the underequipped Peruvian-Bolivian army was defeated by Chilean forces, resulting in the annexation of Bolivia's maritime provinces. The loss of a port condemned Bolivia to landlocked isolation and became a rallying cry for future nationalists. Whether Mollendo specifically created this photograph for propaganda purposes is not known, but it was widely used for that end.

To neutralize or even deny the presence of poor and unemployed in their midst, members of the elite typically ignored them, declaring them, in a way, psychologically invisible. Photograph captions illustrate a variation of this form of denial, either trivializing social conditions, or ignoring them. So photographs of homeless child-beggars are labelled "Ragamuffins Looking for Trouble"; a frightened Indian child's

caption is "The Indian: Soul of America."[12] Traveling foreign photographers and travel writers patronized the poor in similar ways.

Were photographs taken a certain way to achieve a desired effect? The civilian candidate for the Brazilian presidency in 1911, Rui Barbosa, championed himself as the candidate of the people. Pro-Rui newspapers published headlines claiming overwhelming public support and frequently printed accompanying photographs of street rallies to prove their assertion. But close counting of onlookers at *civilista* rallies shows that the crowds were generally sparse. Photo 3.7 depicts a larger crowd than most photographs published during the campaign, but examination of other versions of the same image reveals that it was cropped at the top to maximize the visual impact of the rally participants grouped around the candidate's portrait. In almost every case photographs of the Barbosa campaign were posed to stretch the truth and to support a campaign myth.[13]

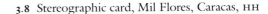

Can a contrived image yield valid evidence? On the other hand, we should be careful not to disregard a visual image simply because it was obviously posed, or because conventions, which are unarticulated understandings, color the visual space. All visual iconography is subjective and rooted in understood convention. Maps always are oriented with north at the top, and with the country of the mapmaker at approximate center. If we identify such conventions and adjust our analysis accordingly, the subject matter need not be prejudiced. The posed conversing figures of the photograph of the Vene-zuelan presidential palace, Mil Flores, hold less interest for us than the room itself (the spittoon on the floor, the statuary mounted on pedestals flanking the doors) because the ornate detail reveals the style of authority of the palace occupants (3.8).

Similarly, *does a photograph record internal as well as external experience?* History and literature record both forms of experience—not just the "fact" of the past but the "feel" of it.[14] The haunting visage of two street vendors in Buenos Aires in the 1860s—possibly by Benito Panunzi—fascinates (3.9). There is evidence that at least one of the sellers was foreign (the newspaper in the basket is in Italian or French). A furtive figure stands behind the glass double doors and there is a flash of movement behind the barred window. Note the indication of the uncomfortable weight of the produce (the strain in the near seller's hands), and the contrasting appearance of the two men's dress: one "Argentine" (note the sash and neck scarf), the other foreign.

The manner in which the men were posed strengthens the visual image. Each of the men, with his two laden baskets, forms a triangle, its base at the ground. Gestalt theory about the ways we see calls this the "law of closure," an ingredient in the creation of visual power.[15]

2. The photographer's intention

How did the photographer approach his subject matter? If we are able to ascertain the empirical preconditions that nourished the photographer's creativity, we will have taken one step toward determining his motives.[16] The American writer and photographer Stephen Crane

3.9 Panunzi?, fruit peddlers, HH

employed his camera to "(expose) the romantic distortions of generations of battle paintings."[17] Of course, we rarely have the opportunity to do this, since we know so little about individual photographers of historical images. Even if we did, there are those who deny any link between who the photographer was and the final print.[18] Sometimes we can guess.

In the following scenes, the first portrays an impromptu shoe market outside of what appears to be a Guadalajaran church: women, some also caring for small children, did the selling (3.10a). In an unattributed photograph of the Isabel la Católica market in Santo Domingo after the turn of the century, the photographer has refused to pose his subjects, capturing them in every form of motion, from stooping down to walking toward the camera; the boy in the hat even has his back to the lens (3.10b). Rarely does a photograph from this period depict daily life in so haphazard a manner. We can surmise that the photographer wanted to record the life of the market itself, not concerning himself with its architecture, the displays of the vendors, or its customers, none of whose faces are captured in the light.

3.10a Dominican Republic market, BV

3.10b Mexican market, UNM

What was the photographer trying to say? Portraits, Oscar Handlin observed, "expose only part of the truth because they reflect the will of the (photographer) as well as the physiognomy of the sitter."[19] Rigid posture, ornate costumes, or special backdrops all contribute to the creation of a distinctive view of the subject, which may or may not ring true historically. Conventions of composition also affect pictorial accuracy. Was the photograph composed in order to portray character, or as background to tell a story?

Constructionists argue that the historical imagination represents a subliminal reflection of contemporary conventions of figurative language and sociocultural conditioning.[20] If so, then the photographer's historical imagination or sense of vision enters each composed image. Look at the purposefulness implied in Samuel Boote's photograph of Buenos Aires's Calle Piedad (circa 1900) (3.11). Well-dressed men and women gather on the narrow sidewalks; traffic is congested, but the central presence of the derbied, cigar-smoking driver lends a feeling of control and nonchalance. The departing trolley is filled with passengers, but not obstructed.

3.11 Boote, Calle Piedad, Buenos Aires, ca. 1900, HH

Men with ponchos over their shoulders stand near the curb, waiting calmly. There is ample evidence of urban prosperity: this clearly is a modern city.

The class and status differences between the photographer and his subject often inserted judgmental elements into the scene. In the same way (although for different motives) Jacob Riis in the United States stigmatized his subjects by dubbing them "the Other Half." However, in the case of Latin American lensmen there was little intention to show suffering or social inequity. Latin American photography aimed at "natural" objectivity, and lacked any element of prescriptive reformism. The fact that most of the members of the Venezuelan fire brigade portrayed in 3.12 are children or youths was not emphasized compositionally in any way by the photographer. The strong visual triangle formed by the two converging lines (and accentuated by the rope) pulls the eye away from the individual figures.

Did the photographer show respect for the subject? Consider the *cartes de visite* depicting Bahian slave women carrying umbrellas on their heads (3.13a and 3.13b). The women are dignified and

3.13a and b Bahian slave woman, GF

well dressed, although both may be wearing the same shawl provided by the photographer. The studio backdrop in the left-hand photograph invokes a rural, outdoors image making the pose, topped by the umbrellas, especially incongruous, perhaps even comical. Even if Afro-Brazilian women carried their umbrellas that way (they did carry many other things on their heads), to the purchasers of the *cartes* the result was probably exotic curiosity, if not ridicule. For what other reasons would collectors pay to acquire such images? The images reveal as much or more about commercial realities faced by photographers in that era than about their subjects.

3. Society's values and norms
How can "official" ideology be distinguished from reality? The top photograph (3.14a) of a rural Brazilian school symbolizes the way in which elites conceptualized the role of charitable institutions run by the state. The photographer's use of a wide lens emphasizes the institutional solidity of the school. Although the people appear as tiny dots below the large central name-

3.14a Exterior of Bahian school, IHB
3.14b Interior of Bahian school, IHB

plate of the building, a further hierarchy of importance is evident: black-suited men in the center (patrons? officials? dignitaries?); women and some children to the side (teachers? pupils?); and on the steps below a collection of less well dressed staff members and children, with a lower-class pedestrian walking by.

If the photograph of the exterior of the Patronato Orphan School boasts of civic virtue, the accompanying photograph of uniformed boys peering anxiously over the oversized wooden desks reveals another, more pathetic side of institutional life (3.14b). The scene is prisonlike and the faces of most of the boys project discomfort and fright. The camera has scrutinized the nameless faces "scientifically," depicting, with cold detail, a supposedly model institution.

How were native people portrayed? As with all portrayals of poor or minority people in Latin America, photographers invariably abstracted them from their lives. The public's fascination with stereotypical ways of seeing Indians led to a predominance of images showing fierce male warriors, nubile young Indian women, or handsome Indian children. In 3.15 Ferrez posed an

aboriginal man with his leg on a rock, his jaw, Prometheus-like, resting on his bent arm. The jaguar skin is dramatically draped and the whole pose suggests primitiveness. At the same time the Indian seems pensive, leaving the viewer puzzled; but the fact that he seems to be cooperating with the cameraman adds a sense of verisimilitude to the scene.

Worst of all, some photographers forced Indian females to pose in entirely unnatural positions, as if they were pinups. Consider the image from a museum collection dating from the 1920s (3.16): the young woman has been asked to strike a pose which conveys indecency to outsiders, but which the photographer may have considered either humorous or fetching.

Some anthropologists spoke out against such degrading portrayals, but to little avail. Everard E. im Thurn, who used photography as part of his field research in Guiana, addressed the Anthropological Institute after returning to London, complaining that poses of native people taken by outsiders were "merely pictures of lifeless bodies," and stating that the "ordinary photographs of uncharacteristically miserable natives . . . seem comparable to the photo-

3.15 Ferrez, seated aborigine, GF

3.16 Indian woman, HH

graphs which one occasionally sees of badly stuffed and distorted birds and animals."[21]

Were photographs used to attribute legitimacy? The work of visiting as well as local photographers was used to lend prestige to political regimes. Eadweard J. Muybridge, the eccentric Englishman trained in San Francisco whose experiments photographing motion brought him worldwide acclaim, traveled as a landscape photographer through Alaska, British Columbia, and Central America in the 1870s.[22] His expenses paid for by the Pacific Mail Steamship Company, Muybridge sailed first to Panama and then to Guatemala, where he spent six months photographing with a large view camera. He was aided by the Guatemalan government, which provided him with unlimited access to sites across the country.[23]

The previous Guatemalan head of state, President-for-life Rafael Carrera, had protected native culture and encouraged the redistribution of former Indian land to Indian communities. The new government, led by positivists, sacrificed Indian autonomy for modernization of the economy through import-substitution and foreign investment in export agriculture.

3.17 Muybridge, Village of coffee pickers at Las Nubes, HH

Having no reason to disagree with the new policy, and needing the income, Muybridge produced stunning compositions showing Guatemala in transition and implicitly endorsing the Liberals' campaign—"the constant march of society toward improvement."[24] Indians, dismissed by the new regime as primitive barbarians and barriers to progress, were portrayed by Muybridge without sympathy (3.17). For the elite, he performed as a welcome agent of change.[25]

A photograph taken by San Martín in Paraguay in 1870 illustrates the lengths to which elites identified personally with the public works projects, which symbolized modernization and progress (3.18). Top-hatted men (engineers? visiting dignitaries?) are posed with three parasoled women (their wives?), with only one shabbily dressed man (at the far right and rear) included to suggest the presence of actual construction workers. Since the "dirty work" of the project was only considered a step en route to the ultimate goal—national progress—it was fitting that the elegantly dressed men and women dominated the photograph's composition.

3.18 San Martín, Caximbu, Paraguay, 1870, HH

3.19a Woman and dead child, ES

3.19b Dead Guatemalan child, TU

Are cultural norms that have changed or vanished depicted? Family photograph albums dating from the nineteenth century frequently contain images of dead children, often in their coffins, usually dressed as angels. Most of the faces of the living in the photographs (usually mothers, fathers, or siblings) are somber but not markedly grieving. This could reflect a combination of reasons, from the fact that the death of children was so commonplace as to be taken in stride, to a possibly unconscious reflex to face the camera in a conventional manner. The mother depicted in 3.19a is dressed in black, her daughter in white, symbolizing that the girl had been baptized and was therefore free from sin. The infant rests with a string of flowers across her forehead, as if she is in a pageant. The photographer's pose ascribes to the mother an air of wistfulness; the position of her hands and arms (and the angle of her head) detracts from the centrality of the child. In another portrait a Guatemalan child is posed in the arms of a plaster angel before she is placed in her coffin (3.19b).

How were crowds portrayed? Perhaps because there was no profit in it, nineteenth-century photographers rarely pointed their lenses at crowded places. As a result, the few surviving images of public rallies and street celebrations deserve examination. A rare photograph by A. Luis Ferreira taken immediately prior to the signing of the bill abolishing slavery (May 13, 1888), records the large crowd waiting outside the palace (the same Paço da Cidade reproduced in the first daguerreotypes) (3.20a). Such scenes were relatively uncommon in the nineteenth century, when officials frowned on crowds as potentially unruly. Ferreira deserves credit for more than simply reproducing a sweeping panorama: he must have appreciated the historical significance of the event and made prior arrangements to photograph it.[26]

Slightly more than three decades later, Jorge Obando captured the momentous public reception for opposition Liberal Party candidates in the Colombian city of Medellín (3.20b). The photograph reproduced here is only *half* of the wide-angle shot of the thousands of well-dressed men and women waiting for the arrival of the visitors. Note not only the two tightly packed groups on the rooftops but the filled windows of the three-story building at center left.

3.20a Crowd outside Paço da Cidade, 13 May 1888, GF

3.20b Reception in Medellín, 1931, ES

Do photographs mislead inadvertently? In a depiction of a near-idyllic scene on a Bolivian river (3.21), a boy stands anchoring his pole in the shallow water; his wide boat—large in contrast to his small stature—is piled with vegetables and a sack, presumably en route to market. The innocent scene makes a simple visual statement about the serene nature of agricultural life. But the image it conveys is historically misleading: it overly romanticizes the pastoral economy by hiding the realities of life in and around Latin American marketplaces. Yet the amateur photographer who captured this scene probably intended no deception: the photograph simply shows a lad in a pleasant, pastoral setting.

What kinds of photographs were produced to assure viewers that society was secure against deviant behavior? Alberto Bixio's photograph of the execution by firing squad of Angel Fernandez, in Montevideo in 1893, was reproduced by the thousands (3.22). Note the uniformed soldiers on the upper rampart, some striking jaunty poses. Behind the line of soldiers in the semicircle around the execution site stands a packed crowd of well-dressed men in civilian attire,

3.21 Boy on river, Bolivia, LG

3.22 Uruguayan execution, 1893, HH

3.23 Troops in Quito street, 1880, HH

3.24 Waiting for General Cipriano Castro, BNC

3.25 Chambi, Policeman and boy, HH

looking as if they were attending a show.

The Latin American military constantly reminded citizens of its presence. In Havana a military band played almost every night in the Plaza de Armas for decades, beginning early in the nineteenth century; the concert, in fact, became a focal point of social life. In 3.23 troops march in the streets of Quito in 1880, fully armed, the fading sun casting long shadows.

Members of the elite welcomed the opportunity to be identified with military figures. Mounted gentlemen form a reception committee for Venezuelan *caudillo* General Cipriano Castro in the 1908 photograph in which the soldiers' placement of their rifles is imitated by at least one dandy with his cane (3.24). Another example of what probably seems to us a mocking juxtaposition of upper-class elegance and military armament is seen in 3.29 (below).

Some decades later, Chambi depicted a policeman grasping an Indian boy by the ear (3.25). The man is in full uniform, his gloves protecting his hands from the dirty urchin he has apprehended. The boy stares at the camera, hunched in pain and humiliation. He is shoeless; the policeman wears shining boots

covered with white leather. The policeman is a mestizo, the ragamuffin an Indian. The cobblestone streets are swept clean, robbing from the scene any visual linkage between the boy and the poverty out of which he obviously came. Posed frontally for documentary emphasis, the image suggests the invisible hand of the elite enforcing law and order through coldly efficient, costumed surrogates. But to Latin Americans of the day the photograph lent reassurance that their world was not to be defiled by deviant or lawless behavior.

*What do photographs documenting political be-
havior or events tell us about societal values and
norms?* The photograph of Quito's presidential
procession (circa 1880) captures the occasion's
quasi-somber mood (in spite of the waving
flags) and illustrates the fact that religious life
was closely intertwined with the secular (3.26).

The posed but nonetheless powerful scene of
Uruguayan soldiers ready to embark via train
evokes a mixture of playfulness (look at the
officer with a beer bottle in his outstretched
hand, and others sipping maté) and gravity
(3.27). That mixed mood is intensified by the
contrasting white in the dresses of the handful
of women accompanying the troops, as if they
were hospital nurses ominously waiting to treat
the wounded and dying.

A rare 1883 photograph of a street barricade
in Quito conveys a sense of ominous potential conflict, even though the severity of the
image is tempered by the relaxed and even
jaunty presence of the two figures in the doorway in front of the barricade and the three
well-dressed men on the balcony (3.28). Perhaps
the conflict has been resolved elsewhere, and
the photographer captures the scene as a state-

3.26 Presidential procession, Quito, 1880, HH

3.27 Uruguayan soldiers and train, HH

ment of civic pride. The massive, improvised roadblock made with paving stones from Incan walls contrasts sharply with the Spanish colonial architecture of the city.

Colombian officers sprawl on the ground in curious ways amidst their weapons and flanked by cannon (3.29). Above them dine elegant gentlemen and ladies at a glittering table, the walls of the large room adorned by flags, banners, and patriotic portraits. Did the photographer seek to convey ridicule, or does the scene reflect the nation's confusion and disorientation from the three-year civil war and its ruinous destruction?

The anonymous Cuban photograph taken after the conclusion of the bloody Ten Years' War (1868–78) delivers a multiracial patriotic message in behalf of the cause of Independence from Spain (3.30). The black rifleman, perhaps a former slave, faces the camera squarely and on equal footing with his three comrades. Although the scene does not mirror Cuba's racial map in any real way, as a propaganda vehicle it delivered a clear messsage.

3.28 Street barricade in Quito, 1883, HH

3.29 Wartime banquet, Colombia, ES

3.30 "Defensores de la Integridad Nacional," Cuba, LC

What does the choice of focal point in landscapes or cityscapes reveal? In both art and photography panoramic vistas, in their iconography, suggest the expectations and functions attributed to them by society. The earliest photographs of Latin American coastal cities almost invariably showed the waterfront; many of the wide-angle views (created by multiple exposures, not wide-angle lenses) were actually shot from boats in the harbor or from offshore bridges, platforms, or islands.

Later in the nineteenth century photographers shifted their vantage points to locales high above and beyond towns and cities, conveying a sense of spatial isolation. Throughout the nineteenth century convention compelled photographers (and artists) to capture, as much as possible, a city as a whole—within a single frame.[27] Sweeping vistas were considered the most desirable, perhaps because of the still fresh fascination with the "scientific" detail possible through photography, or because the distant vantage point lent dignity to the cityscape, distilling noise and movement into a topographical configuration of pattern and order. A further artistic reason was that many photographers

3.31 Panoramic view of Acambaro, Mexico, CMP

3.32 "Una Estancia," Argentine gauchos, HH
3.33 Montevideo bandstand, ca. 1900, HH

were influenced by nineteenth-century land-scape painters—Turner, Constable, the impressionists—who championed pastoral beauty. Cities seemed to violate virtually every artistic convention relating man to his environment.[28] One way to overcome this visual prejudice was to use distance to soften urban sprawl. Adding picturesque figures to the foreground helped even further, as in the Mexican vista of the town of Acambaro (3.31).

4. Probing unstated norms
Does the photograph reveal overt or covert culture? Overt culture designates explicit patterns, presumably understood by the actor and the observer in the same conscious way (Collingwood's "outside events"). Covert culture is composed of implicit patterns formulated by the observer to explain behavior manifested but not explicitly recognized by the actors.[29] Boote's photograph of Argentine gauchos sipping maté alongside the abandoned carcasses of cattle killed only for their hides and more desirable meat (especially the tongue) illustrates the second (covert) instance (3.32): it is unlikely that the cowboys considered their practice an exam-

3.34 Posadas pier, Montevideo, HH

ple of reckless waste, as we would today.

Culture in the United States cloaked interested motives in the language of equity while the structure of privilege remained unnamed.[30] In Latin America elites openly took pride in the symbols of power and privilege. The photograph of pedestrians walking in front of a bandstand in Montevideo, circa 1900, shows the "British Protestant character of the city," which the elites, perhaps unconsciously, were trying to promote (3.33).[31] A second photograph, "Footing," taken at the Posados Beach pier, also in Montevideo, shows the elite taking the sun in full Sunday regalia (3.34).

Does a photograph reveal unstated purposes? Each culture and each period treats perspective, line, composition, and so on from its own world outlook.[32] European and North American social documentarists imposed order on their human subjects to emphasize their poverty, or posed them to suggest certain behavioral traits. Buildings, too, can be photographed differently for different purposes: they can be made to appear central, or can be set so far back that they appear to be receding into the sky.[33]

3.35 Lima, ca. 1882, HH

3.37 Morro do Castello, 1893, HH

3.36 "Homem de Ascendência Negra," IJN

Photo 3.35 dramatically portrays Lima as a sprawling city. The city itself is washed out by sunlight and haze, while the centrally posed black cannon on its revolving platform, and the surrounding soldiers and other bystanders, draw the viewer's attention. Below the man standing at dead center is the city's bullring. The way the photograph was taken is analogous to the shooting of a portrait through a net or with transparent ointment on the lens to soften facial lines. Cities were photographed in ways that hid their blemishes.

Is there information about racial status? The ornate frame (hardwood mounting, gilded filigree border, gold-painted buttons, collar and rings, silk lining) protecting a portrait of an elegantly dressed young black man strongly suggests status and power (3.36). What makes the circa 1860 photograph hard to decipher is that it is from a private collection housed in Recife and carries an understated descriptive caption ("Man of Negro Ancestry"), which probably was added years later. Since there is no evidence that the portrait was ever published, we can assume that the photographer sold it to his client, making it unreasonable for us to read meaning into the caption. Even so, the image carries a strong message. The subject's eyes are closed (because of the long exposure?); his formal dress complements the elegance of the frame and his body confronts the lens squarely, without docility. The man may have been a manumitted former slave living in a part of Brazil with virtually no blacks of even moderate social standing. We are left to speculate.

The photograph of army fortifications during the 1893 Naval Revolt combines contrived posing (the officer wielding his binoculars, bizarrely off to the side) with candid poses (the enlisted men, blacks, stare at the camera) (3.37). Many sailors in the Brazilian navy in the early 1890s were former slaves, freed only a few years earlier. The troops are black, their noncommissioned superior a mulatto, and the officer white. Observe the contrast between the baggy, unkempt uniforms of the soldiers and the tailored jacket of the popinjay officer; and between the officer's asserted vigilance and the look of discomfort in the faces of the two men standing with their backs to the cannon.

Since photographs are documents of a particular era, what was that era's state of mind? Consider Muybridge's photograph of Guatemalan coffee pickers at dinner on an Antiguan hacienda (3.38). Viewing the photograph today evokes harsh images of paternalism and exploitation. The hacienda (or overseer's) family stands along the balcony of the residence, posing for the camera in European dress, apparently ignoring the huddled clusters of workers below. Two other figures, men in white, sit off to the side; it seems that they, too, are superior in status or power to the workers, who are shoeless, dressed in ragged clothing, and squatting in the dirt.

But viewers of the photograph probably thought that the image confirmed the government's success at creating a stable economic base rooted in coffee plantation agriculture. It was seen in a paternalistic context, suggesting welfare and order, not poverty or humiliation. "One cannot help feeling astonished at (the) present social progress (of the current regime)," a European visitor was quoted as saying, "in comparison with the days of Carrera."[34]

What evidence do images provide about foreign influence? An 1865 photograph of Panama's Grand Hotel, by G. E. Fabre, shows a massive European-style building with shingled roofs

3.38 Muybridge, Antiguan hacienda, HH

3.39 Fabre, Grand Hotel, Panama, HH

3.40 Fredricks, Hotel Telégrafo, Havana, HH

and small windows on the upper floors—surely more appropriate for a temperate climate—and English language signs at street level and on the adjacent building (3.39). Except for the mountains in the background, for the most part hidden, there is no evidence whatsoever that this photograph was taken in the torrid, subtropical Isthmus of Panama.

The photograph of Havana's Hotel Telégrafo (1857), attributed to Charles De Forest Fredricks's Havana studio, depicts several levels of activity (3.40). The lettering on the building's facade illustrates an early example of tourist-driven linguistic accommodation: the name is in English at the most prominent place, and in Spanish in a secondary location. Note the 35-star American flag. Was there a consular office here? Were the guests visitors from the United States? On the first balcony gather men in top hats and formal coats and elegant white-gowned women carrying sun umbrellas. Less well dressed men and women (servants?) watch from the upper balcony, whose floor is underlined by the Spanish version of the hotel's name. The drivers sit out of view below; a lone figure (a hotel detective? Fredricks?) stands tall below, and the street is unpaved and filled with stones.[35]

3.41 Argentine gauchos, HH

Does the photograph reveal something society chose to deny? Photo 3.41 shows two gauchos at rest. Both are dressed in traditional gaucho garb, which to us seems ornate but which was worn at least some of the time. The bearded man holding his maté gourd is Caucasian, but his companion is black. A good number of Argentine gauchos were black, just as were many cowboys in the American West. Most Argentine history books have suppressed this fact, and more than one such volume printed this photograph with the black gaucho cropped out.

5. Depiction of social relationships

How did people conceive of themselves? We can discover the answer to this by examining the meaning that was ascribed to the experience of having one's picture taken. Being photographed was an event, novel and memorable. The ways people sat or stood before the camera reveal something about the way they thought about themselves.[36] The first photographic portraits, of course, were versions of painted portraits, available only to members of the elite and sought after as a means to reinforce "social status, economic class, and the institution of the family—more particularly that of matrimony."[37] When photography became accessible to upwardly aspiring members of the middle classes they adopted the same uses for their portrait images. Virtually everyone, regardless of social status, respected the camera's authority.

Consider the startling photograph of prisoners taken four years after the end of the Paraguayan War by a Spanish-speaking photographer (3.42).[38] Both prisoners and guards stare at the camera in exactly the same way, although the prisoners are seated and shackled in leg and arm irons, while the guards stand. The prisoners seem almost polite; some are smiling, even though the convicted murderers are due to be executed within hours. If one considers only the faces of the prisoners, there is nothing that suggests fear, or bravado, or any other emotion which could be construed as out of the ordinary. What kind of power did the camera wield to result in such compliance, beyond a possible sense of resignation under the shadow of the gallows?

An anonymous Colombian photographer recorded the arrest of Quintin Lame and his bandit gang in 1930 (3.43). Not only does the photograph provide marvelous detail—the men's straw capes for camouflage, for example —but it suggests camaraderie, even festivity. The gang leader sits smoking a cigar. A soldier rests his hand on the prisoner's shoulder, not in a pose of restraint but almost of friendship. None of the soldiers' rifles point towards the prisoners, who, it seems, could walk away if they wanted to. There is no clue as to whether the dog belonged to the bandits or to the pursuing militia men.

3.42 Prisoners awaiting execution, BK

3.43 Bandit captured in Colombia, ES

What was the relationship between photographer and subject? Do rigidly composed scenes imply intimidation? Do the subjects relate to one another or individually to the camera? Poses not only describe; they measure comfortableness, authority, and the social distance between photographer and subject.[39] Contrast *carte de visite* images of men and women on the fringes of acceptable society to the relaxed images of socially skilled members of the affluent classes.

The masterful Chambi photograph of a ranch owner and his men depicts a kaleidoscope of hierarchical behavior (3.44). The rancher stands as if he were posing alone. He is aloof, set off by his distinctly formal suit and hat as well as by his posture. In the row immediately behind him stand Indian members of a musical troupe, some ill at ease, others stiffly smiling. The second man from the left is not an Indian; his stance conveys arrogance and a measure of disdain. To the side and front of the ranch owner two unexplained figures squat together: one, a woman, seems to console the man, who gives the appearance of discomfort or possibly even grief. The bottom row is composed of Indian musicians holding primitive-appearing instru-

3.44 Chambi, "Los Q'orilasos de la Provincia de Chumbivilcas," MC

ments crafted from animal horns. Two of the cowboys (one being one of the few Caucasians in the photograph) lie arrogantly on the ground in full costume.

The top row is composed of cowboys in different guises holding ropes, which contrast sharply with the musical instruments held by the men beneath them. Several sit on the railing, one precariously in a swaggering, open-legged pose, his adjacent companion peering directly at the camera, his arms resting on the men to either side. Hand and arm positions in this photograph are odd. The musicians, fingering their instruments, convey a sense of timidity; the ill-dressed overseer type menaces with his crossed arms; the man at upper left has his hand over his heart and the younger man adjacent to him has his cupped over his groin. It seems as if these men are mocking the photographer, who, as an Indian, was vulnerable to disrespect.

How do members of different social groups relate to one another? In Cuzco, the urban center of the region adjacent to the abandoned Incan ruins at Macchu Picchu, six rural men sit on a bench (3.45). They may be waiting for a magis-

3.45 Indians on bench, MC

trate, or hoping for an audience with a bureaucrat. Their acute discomfort is contrasted by the bored faces of the other occupants of the room, all of whom are dressed in European style and obviously familiar with proceedings.

3.46 Carnival in Santiago de Cuba, MP

A small group of white Cuban revellers in the late 1920s step out into the street dressed as women (3.46). They seem self-conscious and are not surrounded by the usual throngs of dancing celebrants, mostly nonwhites, who typically dominate Carnival. A mestizo walks beside them looking at the camera, but he is not part of their group. The photograph is taken from a family album of Sephardic Jewish emigrants to Cuba from Turkey. These, then, are immigrants whose celebration is shared neither by the upper-class Cubans in their private clubs, nor by the majority of the lower-class population. They were probably on their way to a private party.

What were the relationships between leaders and followers? In 1945 Víctor Raul Haya de la Torre and his Apra party were banned from formal participation in that year's elections. But Haya, the founder and leader of Peru's first major populist movement, campaigned vigorously for the Frente Democrático Nacional, expecting to play a role in the next government. The photograph in 3.47 shows him leaning over to allow a peasant to kiss his hand at a campaign stop in

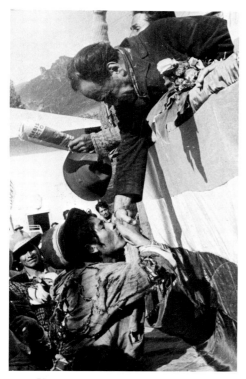

3.47 Haya de la Torre, ss

3.48 Guajiro cacique, ES

the city of Huancayo. The way in which the hierarchical relationships are literally depicted is striking. Haya, positioned above his followers, physically reaches down to make contact. Thus the scene replicates the traditional vertical relationship of patrimonial politics characteristic of much of Latin America in the early twentieth century. Haya holds out his hand to be kissed in the style, perhaps, of Peru's colonial viceroys, whose contacts with the masses largely took the form of public audiences. For his part, the peasant makes a show of deference, a central element of his own political behavior, demonstrating that the superior is owed deep respect but, at the same time, is personally approachable.[40]

In 1909 an unknown photographer captured two Guajiro Indians, one of them a tribal *cacique*, holding up a portrait of Colombia's President Reyes (3.48). Two different levels of hierarchy are depicted. The clothing worn by the *cacique* and his wife, especially the woman's embroidered *manto*, affirms the couple's status. The photograph documents the political system based on *caciquism:* the local chieftain's power is derived directly from the patronage of the national chief, whose portrait is held as if it were a saint's image.[41]]

6. Everyday life

Do photographic images penetrate posed decorum? Elites attempted to act as dignified and ceremonious as possible, even if once in a while reality intruded, as in the case of the delightfully inadvertent glimpse of two curious children behind the ornate, classical set in the studio of Revert Henrique Klumb, circa 1855 (3.49).

Simple country dwellers were depicted in ways emphasizing their passivity rather than their impoverishment. This was done to protect viewers from the worst of reality. When photographers did reproduce images of poverty, whether urban or rural, they employed visual devices to distract the viewer and to minimize evidence of suffering, conflict, and militancy. Subjects were carefully chosen to reflect this view. Photo 3.50, taken in the Dominican Republic in 1915 or 1916 by a photographer accompanying scientists from the American Museum of Natural History, is captioned in English, "Traditional Hospitality." The Caucasian woman, probably an outsider, wears shoes; the others are barefoot. Most of the subjects are wearing filthy clothing. But the camera focuses on the china cup of coffee offered to the guest, and on the pipes smoked by the black man and woman. The final result is a composition that fits the caption and which suggests that the viewer ignore the evidence of squalor that permeates the scene.

What is the evidence of material culture? The most useful of such visual data are objects incidental to the primary subject in the composition. What is the proportion of nonutilitarian objects to utilitarian objects?[42] What do the number and placement of objects reveal? What is the meaning of the man-made order which photographs often show? The print, circa 1880, by the German-Chilean Heffer, of an Araucanian native dwelling offers a wealth of detail for analysis, including food, storage utensils, weaving equipment, fabrics, skins, furniture, and house construction, although the photographer was probably more interested in the human subjects (3.51).

How did people live and die? A 1914 photograph by Hugo Brehme captures a poignant side of war. Captioned "Pancho Villa's Soldiers," it shows a huddled collection—mostly men and children—traveling (or camped out) on top of

3.49 Klumb, woman and two children, GF

3.50 "Traditional Hospitality," BV

3.51 Heffer, Araucanian hut interior, HH

a boxcar in an urban district, possibly Mexico City (3.52a). Only one man, to the back of the picture, wears a uniform. The clothing bundles, cooking utensils, umbrellas, boxes, baskets, and sacks strewn across the top of the car, and the small groups of people huddled in their midst, add up to a very convincing image.

The Mexican "Paupers' Funeral Tram," a closed boxcar holding eight adult coffins (or sixteen of child size), made stops at street corners for loading (3.52b). Once filled the cart was taken to the cemetery at top speed, where the corpses were dumped into open, common graves. The empty boxes were reloaded on the funeral car for rerental.

How did people pose for the camera? Family photographs mirror not only broad conventions of society, but also the personal aesthetic and social conventions of the individuals who take them, pose, and save them. They are particularly interesting when they include symbols of status; images of family members posed in front of houses, or within comfortable rooms, suggest spatial mastery, an attributed harmony of people to setting. Family portraitists have borrowed, knowingly or not, from the Dutch masters. Recall Van Eyck's "Betrothal of the Arnolfi" (1434), for example: the couple is surrounded by a meticulous household inventory —windows, shutters, a mirror, shoes, a dog, emblems of prayer.[43] Photographers of Latin America's comfortable families surrounded their subjects with property—furniture, pianos, vases, lace tablecloths, religious statuary. Even in photographs of family groups on the frontier, the subjects are often surrounded with material possessions, or are posed outside of their houses amidst their horses, carts, domestic animals, and farm implements.

Who sat (or stood) at the center of the composition, a placement indicating authority or respect? Who stood at the periphery? Were servants included in family portraits and if so, in what compositional relation to family members? Do people seem relaxed or stern? Do they touch in any way? Does the clothing match the social setting? Since studio photographers commonly provided elegant finery for subjects as part of the posing fee, photographs taken outside of the studio would seem to speak more authentically about clothing. The way individuals in photographs were dressed was extremely

3.52a Brehme, Boxcar, AM
3.52b Mexican pauper's funeral tram, UNM

3.53a Elite family, ES

3.53b Elite young women, ES

important in the nineteenth and early twentieth century, since as geographic mobility and immigration increased, photographs provided ways to communicate personal well being over distances.

The poses in the next three photographs are clearly meant to convey a message. A Colombian family sits for their studio portrait around the turn of the century, obviously proud of themselves (3.53a). Four young women strike mock adventuresome poses; the way they hold their rifles adds to the spoof (3.53b). A Cuban family in the courtyard of their home is photographed vertically to include a second level of onlookers, presumably servants, above (3.53c). Below, in the lap of comfort, sits the head of the household holding a cigar, his feet on a chair.[44]

How is status conveyed? Photo 3.54 is from preabolition rural Brazil; it vividly portrays the status roles within a family environment. The man sits mounted on his horse, overshadowing and even obscuring members of his own family and the household's slaves. His head is framed by the dark doorway, making his portrait all the more vivid in contrast to the obscured faces of

3.53c Cuban family in courtyard, RF

3.54 Mounted planter, GMS

most of the others. Apparently, little effort was made to pose the other subjects. The most important figure here is the man and horse; the next is the groom holding the reins. The family dog is centered below the horse, given a more prominent place in the photograph than the slave children, hidden under and behind the horse, and the women. All of this adds up to a powerful display of egoism, even to the stiffness of the rider's arm, which holds a whip, and half-grimace with which he stares off to the side, not facing the lens.

Do individuals captured in a relaxed state show behavior or a frame of mind differing from socially expected traits? One sphere in which photographs recorded relaxation was sports. Baseball players who otherwise were *henequén* field workers in the Yucatán in the 1920s are lined up in 3.55. For the most part they were *milperos*, maize-growing peasants, who played in leagues on Sundays wearing makeshift uniforms or even their traditional white *traje* and field aprons.[45]

What clues do facial expression and body language offer about status and self-image? It has been said that most men and women who pose for the camera put on the face they would like

to show the world.[46] A Venezuelan couple pose stiffly for the camera: the man, older, sits with an air of authority; his younger wife leans on his shoulder, perhaps symbolizing the relationship (3.56).

An altogether different anonymous photograph of Indian women and an interloper dressed in a business suit, taken around 1930 in Patagonia, offends us (3.57). This is not because of the expression on the man's face, which is neutral (is he more interested in posing for the lens than in the young women, despite his prurient behavior?) The native women are clearly uncomfortable. They cover their genitals with their hands; none looks directly at the camera, and at least three of the four appear ashamed. The man's arms are (casually?) draped around two of the women; his right hand cradles a breast, almost reaching the nipple. The caption is blunt: "Naked Indians with Visiting Anthropologist."

What do photographs reveal about customs and dress? An anonymous print from the mid-1860s, "House of the British Minister, Bogotá, Colombia," shows a rare glimpse of working stagecoaches (3.58). Both drivers are wearing

3.55a and **b** Baseball players, GJ

3.56 Venezuelan couple, BNC

the clothing of Indians in the Andean region —ponchos, hats, and sandals—while the bystanders wear the standard western garb used by Europeans throughout the continent. The upper balconies of the handsome residence are draped with flowering plants, an unexpected sight, and a man stands at the main balcony in a formal top hat. On the sidewalk at the right side of the house there is a blurred, partially supine figure—probably a man but possibly an animal (a small mule)? The coach passengers wait patiently. All are well dressed and in brim hats. There is an open sewer running across the street, which is partially paved over in front of the lead carriage.

A family portrait, dated 1908, from Paraíba do Norte in Brazil, depicts a traditional upper-class family; the father was a leading businessman (3.59). The boy at the right of the picture is dressed in a full-length clerical habit, although he is likely no more than ten years of age. It was the custom of families to send youths to church schools, but the use of the priest's garb rather than a simple school uniform implies that the boy planned to pursue the priesthood.

3.59 Brazilian family with acolyte, 1908, IJN

7. Unexpected or suppressed information
Is there unexpected visual detail? In the photograph taken by the German August Riedel on an expedition through Brazil's mining region with the Duke of Saxe in 1868, the large cross in front of the Aquetiba Church in Rio das Velhas is decorated with more than a dozen unlikely objects (3.60a). Lowest on the vertical post is a skull and crossbones. Above the skull are two unidentifiable objects, the uppermost one perhaps with symbolic eyes. On the horizontal post are mounted a number of tools and implements, including pliers, hammers, and sickles, framed on each end by a hanging tassel. The scale of the elements in the composition lends a sense of bleakness: the building and cross so overwhelm the tiny human onlookers.

The artifacts represent a local variant of the *ex voto* phenomenon of Brazilian syncretistic folk Catholicism; but these were almost always carved representations of human body parts (usually heads or limbs afflicted by disease for which the penitent sought a cure), not the articles represented here. That the Minas Gerais region is considered to have been the most devoutly orthodox home of Brazilian Catholi-

3.60a Reidel, Church, Minas Gerais, 1868, GF

3.60b Occupation soldier, Peru, AM

cism makes the visual information provided here seem even more odd.

An anonymous Peruvian photographer posed a member of the occupying Chilean army, after the War of the Pacific, sharing a pedestal with a wine bottle and glass (3.60b). Was the photographer mocking the foreigners?[47]

Does secondary detail provide information that contrasts with the primary object of interest? The Marc Ferrez photograph of the dedication of the Mantiqueira Railroad Tunnel was intended primarily to show the dignitaries and officials, including Brazil's imperial family, at the entrance (3.61). All of the figures at the tunnel's mouth are formally dressed and obviously carefully posed. The top of the tunnel has been covered with layers of palm fronds, presumably to hide the loose dirt, but visually this acts to separate the figures at the bottom from onlookers at the top. Ferrez probably used vertical framing to add a further dimension of scale and height to his composition. In so doing he included at the top a second level of onlookers, some well dressed, others with open jackets (and darker complexions), probably workers or nearby residents. The presence of the construc-

3.62 Patagonian Indians, EW

tion shack at top left adds to the realism of this photograph. The movement among the figures at the top level contrasts with the stillness and sharp detail of the standing figures at bottom, who were posed carefully by the photographer.

Does the photograph reveal telling emotion? Look at the disorientation in the faces of the Patagonian Indians photographed by members of an Argentine army expedition to the south in the early 1900s (3.62). The blurred movement of the subjects and the camera's low angle add to the sense of uneasiness.

3.63 Indians, HH

3.64a Ferrez, Port of Santos, HH
3.64b La Boca docks, Buenos Aires, HH

In 3.63 the Indians in the top row do not seem to be unduly intimidated: one man impatiently crosses his arms. But the women and children kneeling in front seem to be miserable. Are their arms wrapped around them for protection, or to cover their emaciated bodies? By squeezing so many people into one frame, the Lima studio photographer Garreaud accentuated the pathos of the scene, although the effect may or may not have been intentional.

Does the image offer clues to unstated circumstances? A forest of ship masts in the Port of Santos near São Paulo in the early 1880s is the clue in 3.64a. Some small boats are being unloaded, but the larger vessels are standing idle at anchor. The inactivity was enforced by medical quarantine. It was common during the nineteenth century, when epidemic disease still ravaged port cities, to intern ship's crews until the spread of a new outbreak subsided. A second photograph, at the La Boca docks in Buenos Aires in 1885, may well show a similar quarantine (3.64b). The presence of standing water suggests that places where mosquitos could breed were widespread. That mosquitoes spread contagion, of course, was not known then.

In 3.65, although the street appears crowded as it recedes from view in the direction of the mountains, the figures in the foreground are obviously posed. A man sits silently on his horse, another leans his saxophone on the cobblestones, and another holds his bass drum. The white-suited man stares directly into the camera, while three other serape-draped figures look to the side, their faces in shadow.

Looking beyond the human figures, the photograph shows us something else. Running down the center of the street, presumably along its entire length, is an open sewer. The water is running enough to make ripples, and here and there is evidence that it is overflowing its banks. Presumably, refuse is tossed into the water's path, which probably floods the entire street in times of heavy rain. The photographer, planning his exposure for sale to armchair stereoscopic tourists, may or may not have considered the sewage canal anything more than a compositional axis that would divide his frame. But as a social document, the photograph remains highly useful as a reminder of unsanitary urban conditions in much of Latin America in earlier decades.

3.67 Emaciated woman and child, LG

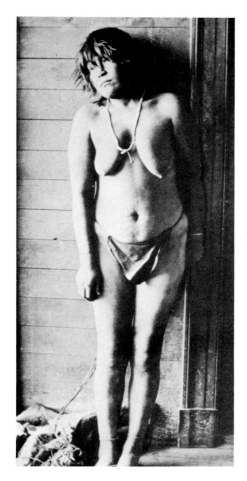

3.66 Indian woman slave, HH

Photographers showed less restraint in depicting the ugly side of life among native peoples, perhaps because they felt morally superior or simply because they considered their Indian subjects exotic. The young Indian woman in 3.66 was photographed in Tierra del Fuego, Chile in approximately 1895. She was probably forced to serve as a prostitute or concubine to white residents: there is a metal bracelet on her left wrist; her robe lies at her feet; and there is a leather cord looped around her throat trailing behind her to the ground. Her facial expression and body stance suggest weary resignation.[48]

A photograph taken in the Chaco by a Bolivian physician accompanying a German medical expedition to the region in 1923, depicts a terrible example of hunger among the people visited by the expedition (3.67). The caption reads: "Indian Encountered 40 Leagues (200 Kilometers) from the Bolivian Fort." Both woman and child are certainly near death; they have the appearance of concentration camp corpses or victims of Ethiopian famine. Although the expedition sought to bring medicine to remote forest areas of Bolivia, there is no evidence of any lasting and systematic institutional effort to deal with the problem. It is telling that while writers on Latin American subjects have long dealt with droughts, forced migrations, war, malnutrition, and social inequities, rarely have they used visual evidence such as this to document what they described.

3.68 Zacotecas market, CMP

Does the presence of detail provide more than the photographer intended? Photo 3.68 is a photograph of an elderly woman sitting before a stall in a market in Zacotecas, Mexico. She is so wrapped in her thin blanket that her face is barely visible. In the background two men watch the camera, yet they do not detract from the woman. The way she is dressed and the manner in which she seems to protect herself from the world (although she is trying to sell the onions spread out before her), is poignant to us because we are concerned about poverty. The photographer, on the other hand, probably was more concerned with recording the market-place.

The Cuzcan scene in 3.69 is evidently posed; some of the men and boys facing the camera are well aware of it. Two musicians at the rear of the courtyard are playing a flute and drum. But beyond this the picture offers a wealth of detail. The men seated at the table are eating from dishes in their laps, almost as if they are afraid to dirty the too small tablecloth, which is covered at its periphery with small rounds of bread. Only one or two women are in view; the woman near the table squats on the floor,

watching the camera with a sense of solemnity or fear—she does not participate in the meal. The two adult male figures in the background wear European clothing, as do three children with them. An abandoned structure sags in the corn field above the wall, which is covered by makeshift roofing tiles. The photograph, by a photographer under contract to Underwood and Underwood, shows men eagerly sating their hunger; it shows poverty (note the barefooted boys in the foreground against the wall); and the gaunt faces and blurred movement of hands to mouths evoke an unnerving sense of stress based on deprivation.

Does the photograph reveal harsh working conditions? A stereographic card from the early 1900s shows Arequipa laborers preparing wool, for which they were paid the equivalent of twenty cents a day (3.70a). The three men in the center atop the tin roof, wretchedly dressed in burlap bags tied with strings, pause timidly in recognition of the photographer's presence. The four men behind them, better dressed in shirts and trousers, continue their work sifting through the strands of raw wool. In the foreground two workers wearing hats and ragged

3.70a and b Stereographic card, Arequipa wool workers, CMP

shirts kneel in a vat of filthy water, oblivious to the camera. And at ground level, on the right, other workers, women, stand over a pile of wool, separating grades with their children at their sides. On the top of one three-foot-high mound covered with burlap, sits a child's wool doll (visible in the second photograph of the indoor working area, 3.70b). Photographs in this series convey unadorned glimpses into working conditions, divisions of labor, and the physical stature of men and women in the rural countryside.

Does the photograph depict artifacts or activities which provoke speculation? Heffer took the photograph of the Indian in an Araucanian burial ground in Chile around 1880 (3.71). The facial expression and pose of his Indian subject—eyes closed, hands outstretched—suggest that he is praying. Some of the grave markers are Christian crosses; others bear a star-shaped pattern that is crosslike but probably pagan.[49] The most arresting aspect of this scene is the odd presence of tall and short markers bearing images of men wearing bowler hats. All of the markers seem weathered and of approximately the same age. Cultural historians and anthropologists can

3.71 Heffer, Araucanian burial ground, HH

cull a wealth of supposition from photographs of this kind.

Do photographs capture misery and suffering? Consider the woeful photograph of women and children who survived the final destruction of Canudos in 1897, when all of the male defenders but four were killed by the attacking Brazilian army (3.72a).[50] The seated figures are dressed grimly in mourninglike garb, which includes head coverings. Some of the children attempt to smile, but the women twist their cupped hands over their faces in a state of shock. This is not the kind of scene that members of the coastal elite ever saw, and it shocked even the observers who justified the campaign against the Canudos peasants on the grounds that they were crazed religious fanatics. A second photograph captures the anguish and exhaustion of the encamped women and their children (3.72b). Most of these women are black; ex-slaves formed a disproportionately high percentage of Canudos's population.[51]

3.72a and **b** Canudos survivors, CEEC

3.73a Araucanian youth, HH
3.73b Guatemalan Indian girl, HH

8. Romanticization

What do poses of idealized types show? When Amerindians were not portrayed as exotic savages, they were often depicted in romanticized poses. Indians appearing in nineteenth-century Latin American literature were frequently described as Ariel-like spirits or as dark-skinned primitives, unable to accept the lighter-pigmented, "civilized" world, and therefore destined to be subjects for curiosity and study before their subcivilized world vanished (see fig. 3.73a and 3.73b).

How did photographers translate social values? Studio photographers relished opportunities not only to confirm but to embellish ways in which society idealized social categories. They were in their element when asked to photograph young women of the elite. Henri Duperly, for example, used a wooden lyre as a prop (3.74). But there may be more than purity and innocence suggested in this portrait. The young woman's eyes coyly avoid the camera; her dress is seductively draped off her shoulder. Was she conveying sexuality offhandedly, or was she coaxed by the photographer? The puzzle is made more complex by the fact that (we know

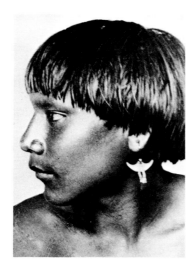

3.74 Duperly, girl with lyre, ES

from the caption) the girl was Duperly's daughter. Young women of the elite did cultivate flirtatiousness at the same time that they projected a purity and innocence. Obviously the photographer did not mind.

9. Satire and irony

What does photographic satire suggest? Especially in the heyday of studio portraiture, men and women sometimes clowned before the camera, even wearing costumes of considerable elaboration. Other photographs, sometimes taken without the consent of the subject, approximate caricature or exaggeration for emphasis. In the example in 3.75, a young man from the elite sits ready to commune with the occult. There is a hooded figure behind him, probably created by a sheet, an Egyptian vase, and an hourglass, all part of the paraphernalia of seances and spiritism which were popular among members of the elite at the time. The subject's relaxed pose and willingness to engage in good-humored playfulness comment on his ease with being captured publicly in a manner that would have scandalized the previous generation.

Some photographers, hemmed in by photographic convention, boldly broke out of the mold by using humor and trick photography to establish themselves as bohemians. What they were trying to do was to gain acceptance as artists, to whom society extended a greater degree of tolerance than photographers. One such photographer was Valério Vieira, an accomplished musician and artist as well as the owner of a photographic studio in São Paulo. His work featuring thirty self-portraits, "The Thirty Valérios," won a silver medal for originality at the St. Louis Exposition in 1901—a breakthrough for the otherwise staid image of Latin American photography (3.76).[52]

What does cliché say about cultural perceptions? "Love-making Cuban Style" (circa 1895), was obviously the work of an English language photographer shooting for the home market (3.77). The young man furtively passes a note to (or receives one from) the heavily chaperoned young woman who, with eyes averted, stands as if in jail. The black nursemaid holding the white child is not barred from the suitor, attesting to her social undesirability. In postcard form these kinds of scenes sold briskly in Cuba as well as abroad. It is anyone's guess as to

3.75 Portrait with "spirit," BK

3.76 Vieira, "The Thirty Valérios," GF

how receptive upper-class Cubans were to such scenes: they may well have considered them funny.

10. Change over time

What changes show in sequences of images photographed over time? Beyond analysis of individual photographs, the historian will find it useful to examine sequences of photographic images over time. Published collections emphasizing evolutionary aspects of Latin American city life have usually focused on architectural and spatial change.[53] Militão de Azevedo's *Album Comparativo da Cidade de São Paulo, 1862–1887* typifies the documentary school. The *Album* offers two sets of street vistas, the first in 1862, the second rephotographed from the same position after a twenty-five year interval (3.78 and 3.79). By the time of the second set his city had been transformed from a muddy provincial capital to a nascent coffee metropolis flexing to dominate regional commerce and industry. The later views present a city which is more livable —landscaped with trees and shrubbery—and with modern features, such as trolley tracks and awnings.[54]

3.77 "Love-making Cuban Style," RF

3.78 Militão de Azevedo, São Paulo, street vistas, 1862 and 1887, HH

3.79 Militão de Azevedo, São Paulo, street vistas, 1862–1887, HH

Still, there were limits. Militão's photo essay depicted few people. Since photographers were mostly interested in documenting material progress, human figures were either excluded from their compositions or rendered incidental. But the photographs are valuable nonetheless. In the late nineteenth century it was still assumed that photographs were first and foremost *pictures*, a "natural" representation identical with the visual impression an observer would get at the same spot as the camera lens.[55] As such, the urban vistas of Azevedo, Gros, Duperly, and their contemporaries hold particular value because they were composed without intent to distort. Perhaps banal, their guilelessness adds a dimension of depth.[56]

It would seem more useful to study the portrayal of a single theme or subject over a period of years or decades, or the output of representative photographers or photographic studios. Applied anthropologists have posited rules to measure well-being (intrinsic care of property, self-expression, visible health) and to inventory cultural experience.[57] Viewing large numbers of photographs offers at least a partial antidote to imbuing images with one's own stereotypes.

Transactional psychologists have shown convincingly that two different viewers of the same event can have strikingly different reactions, seeing different things. Examining dozens and even hundreds of photographs of like subjects can help us form a more intense comparative view based on similarities and differences. This in turn permits us to see cultures on their own terms.

The process used to create a photograph —the passing of reflected light through a lens and onto a light-sensitive surface—naturally influenced the way viewers perceived photographs. Observers in the western visual tradition expected photographs to explain and assumed that the subjects framed at the center of the composition were significant. The photographer's camera, John Tagg reminds us, is focused on "a world of objects already constructed as a world of uses, values, and meanings, though in the perceptual process these may not appear as such but only as qualities discerned in a 'natural' recognition of 'what is there.'"[58] The Cuban photograph dating from the late 1850s, captioned "Negro in Stocks," is too static and lifeless not to have been staged

(3.80). The man's feet lie across the aperture of the stock, but the iron clamp used to seal it lies open at the side. This is not the point, however. The practice's inherent cruelty is what offends our eye today; but for the contemporary viewers of this image, the scene may well have been considered one of several depictions of "local color." After all, in the 1850s slavery in Cuba was still fully lawful. The way the photograph was posed tells us about the cold-blooded neutrality of the photographer's eye and, as such, about the point of view of the age in which it was taken.

Photo 3.81 was not a contrived photograph. A shoeless Chinese coolie laborer on a Peruvian sugar cane plantation in Chicamita stands facing the camera, his legs restrained by heavy metal fetters linked to his ankles and waist. Chinese laborers were imported after abolition and were photographed for identification, lest they run away. Presumably, this man had so attempted. This kind of evidence rarely appears in history books, although this particular photograph was published in a presentation album, *Republica Peruana 1900*, which was presumably intended as a record of progress.[59] Contempo-

3.80 Negro in stocks, HH

rary viewers probably did not view the photograph as we do today.

Photographs may be used to question stereotypes, even those which have been absorbed into national mythology. Samuel Boote's studies of life on the Argentine pampa during the last quarter of the nineteenth century strip gaucho life of undue glamor. The ranching couple of 3.82 lived in a mud hut; here they are surrounded by turkeys and sheep. The woman holds her teapot; a child lingers behind her. At the edge of the picture stands an older youth dressed as a horseman; the way he holds his feet suggests boredom, not derring-do.

A black female slave carries a heavy wooden box of prepared food on her head while a companion with Caucasian features stands facing the camera (3.83). The black slave faces away from the camera, in humility, while the girl stands her ground with an air of impatience. The photographer, Augusto Stahl, captioned his composition "sellers." Was he trying to convey a sense of unequal racial status, or did the girl pose assertively on her own because of a more confident personality?

3.81 Coolie, Peru, IRPB

3.82 Boote, Mud hut on Argentina pampa, HH

3.83 Stahl, Sellers, GF

3.84 Ferrez, Gold miners, GF

Marc Ferrez's photograph of the interior of a gold mine taken around 1880 dramatically documents the resident dangers of the work and the strenuous lot of the laborers (3.84). The men's backs, some muscular and glistening with sweat, and their vertical positioning on the rock face lend dramatic compositional quality to the image, the bodies forming part of the latticework of wooden poles, ropes, and makeshift platforms. Ferrez's decision to use the miners as part of his composition, and to shoot at their backs, lends strength to his image but renders the men literally faceless. The photograph shows no interest in them as human beings; they are not recognized for their individual dignity.

THE POSED world created by photographers in nineteenth- and early twentieth-century Latin America consisted of subjects framed according to conventionally accepted ways of seeing. Studio poses provided the sitter a special space "with which to compose himself into an expression, a *picture*, that approximates his own as well as his society's ideal."[1] Unposed images—formal photographs gone wrong, snapshots of momentary encounters, people standing at the periphery of scenes focusing on other subjects, or subjects taken straight on, without contrivance or prompting—offer a sharply contrasting vision.

This chapter groups such images, comparing the artifice consonant with social myth (I) to the real world of everyday circumstance (II). One must use caution: the line between "posed" and "unposed" may be narrower than expected. Spontaneity, after all, may in some cases be as much of a pose as a pose.[2] On the other hand, all images, particularly candid ones created quickly, allow us to learn not only about them but about ourselves as well.

Slaves (I)

Photographers usually took pains to avoid moralizing content when using slaves as their subjects. In the 1882 Ferrez view of field hands gathering coffee on a hillside, the figures seem to belong to the land itself (4.1). In the midst of the slaves, mostly obscured in his dark jacket, stands a black overseer with whip in hand. The slaves work in rows oriented up the hillside, which prompted soil erosion but which made surveillance easy. Whatever Ferrez was trying to convey, the effect of the patterned composition and the distance from the lens imposes a peaceful, even serene effect on a scene documenting a harsh workday of fourteen to fifteen hours.

A second Ferrez image, of another coffee plantation, captures the same kind of stately formality horizontally, as if the slaves were performing a kind of agricultural ballet (4.2). In neither picture do we see any individual closely enough to distinguish one from another; the subjects are subservient to the theme—the picturesque quality of rural life. Fredricks's posed Cuban sugar cane harvest (see 4.50 below) obeys the same formula. The view is utopian. The fields are depicted as if they were model

workplaces, a plantation version of Jeremy Bentham's Panopticon, in which all inmates would be constantly exposed to the view of others.[3]

Slaves (II)

A contrasting view of plantation work, also by Ferrez, allows the individual slave hands to dominate the image (4.3). What strikes the eye is how short they are, and how their faces and slumped physiognomies convey weariness. The slaves include at least two women and several adolescents; the young woman at center is visibly pregnant. The overseer may have ordered his slaves to wear their Sunday clothes for the camera (an attempt at "dressing up" the portrait), but they are still barefoot, subject to the constant threat of parasitic infection.[4]

When examining 4.4, think about the caption—"*The* Master and His Slaves" (not "*A* Master and His Slaves"). Also, note the way the white man stands alone in front of the others. He is portly and partially blocks our view of the two men behind him. The slaves do not appear intimidated, but the way the scene is posed

4.1 Ferrez, Coffee workers. GF

4.2 Ferrez, Coffee workers, GF

4.3 Ferrez, Tired plantation workers, GF

4.4 "The Master and His Slaves," BK

there is no doubt about their servility and the master's supremacy. This is a frank portrait, as are the next two photographs.

In 4.5 (circa 1855) a Bahian slave woman wears silver bracelets and heavy rings. These represent all of her worldly possessions; they will be sold at her death to pay for her burial. A black man (photographed by Christiano Júnior during the 1850s) stands posed in front of a wall, but he is given enough latitude to assert his own personality (4.6). He offers the camera a weary look. Barefoot and carrying a basket that is obviously heavy when full, he is clearly shown to be a slave.

A young flour sifter stands naked except for a loincloth (4.7). Behind his legs (and possibly attached to one ankle) a set of iron fetters provides an unforgettable reminder of his status. A woman whose face bears African tribal markings hands a fruit to a boy (4.8). Is he her son? Or is he posed to represent a slave lad, sent out to market to fill his small basket with fruit? A young woman is posed naked from the waist (4.9). She seems docile, almost relaxed before the camera. Christiano Júnior, the photographer, almost always presented his subjects with

4.5 Bahian slave woman, HH

4.6 Christiano Júnior, Black slave, FN

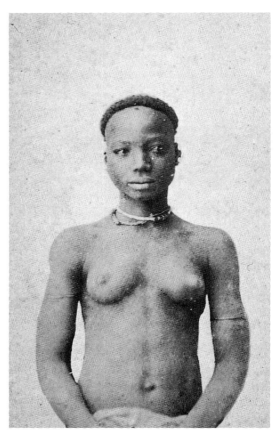

4.7 Christiano Júnior, Slave flour sifter, FN

4.8 Christiano Júnior, Slave woman with fruit, FN

4.9 Christiano Júnior, Naked girl slave, FN

4.10 Christiano Júnior, Slave couple, FN

4.11 Christiano Júnior, Crippled slave, FN

dignity, so it is hard to understand why he produced this *carte de visite* in a frontally nude pose. Did he do this for commercial motives, or was he naively attempting to capture the young woman's attractiveness?[5] In any case, the degradation to which blacks were subject under slavery is clearly transmitted in this, as well as the previous two photographs.

Another upsetting image, although in a lower key, is the posed portrait of a man and woman and their wares in 4.10. The man's once elegant frock coat and trousers are so ill fitting and tattered that the otherwise seriousness of the composition is marred by a sense of visual pathos. Or did purchasers of this *carte de visite* laugh? In 4.11 a man poses with his wooden prosthesis; he leans on a cane. He too must stand in the street and sell. Was he selected as a subject because of his "human interest"? He does not appear to be very comfortable before the lens.

Commerce (I)

The covered shopping arcade in 4.12, taken in Santiago around 1900, is clean, polished, and orderly. There are few customers; it is siesta hour. White-aproned shop employees (and some shop owners?) stand in front of their doorways. There are no women in the photograph. At first glance, the man facing the camera in a bowler hat looks like a policeman, but he is simply wearing a dark, fitted suit. The only other figures in the photograph are well-dressed shopkeepers and upper-class buyers. The high, vaulted, glass-enclosed ceilings and the physical setting was obviously the photographer's first priority.

Commerce (II)

Photo 4.13 shows a marketplace in Chillán, Chile, from the same period. There is a wealth of animals, carts, wooden structures, merchandise, and people, even places to eat and for entertainment. In the lower portion of the photograph a man has set up six chairs for spectators to watch him perform.[6] An even more primitive rural *feria*, or market, takes place in the Dominican Republic around 1908 in 4.14. Only a few wooden structures stand; most of the vendors sit on the ground, which is rough and muddy. These two photographs convey the real experience of the marketplace—a center of teeming activity.

4.12 Arcade, Santiago, HH

4.13 Chilean marketplace, HH

4.14 Marketplace, Dominican Republic, BV

The Military (I)

Spaniard Juan Gutiérrez, who later would become possibly the first photographer to die during military hostilities (at Canudos), photographed a contingent of Brazilian army troops in Rio de Janeiro (4.15). A stern man in civilian clothing faces the searchlight; an officer with crossed arms faces the other way, and soldiers wearing light-colored uniforms stand uneasily at the back. The lifeless poses give the scene little authenticity, although it was photographed in the midst of the 1893 Naval Rebellion.

A second photograph, by A. Malta and dated 1930, shows the São Paulo State Militia en route to encampment (4.16). It parodies military discipline. The rifles point every which way; two soldiers even aim their rifles at comrades. Yet within two years the *paulistas* would initiate a civil war against the national government, a matter which was deadly serious. The photograph could not have helped improve the generally low esteem in which foot soldiers were held.

In 4.17 a fat Mexican general stands on the

4.15 Brazilian troops, 1893 Naval Revolt, HH

running board of his American sedan, obtained in El Paso. The automobile is obviously a prized possession. Interestingly, although the photographer probably did not intend it as such, the anomalous basketball backboard lends additional emphasis to the theme of material wealth.

4.16 São Paulo State Militia, HH

4.17 Mexican general, CMP

The Military (II)

Other photographs show a more authentic sense of military presence, even though we know that one (4.18), by Uruguayan Jesús Cubela, was staged: an Indian woman holding a long knife stands in front of the regular cavalry on exercise, circa 1870. Parading troops marching down a Mexico City street attract so little attention that almost no one in the photograph bothers to look at them (4.19). Indeed, the only person pointing is a small boy who is pointing to something else. In the third photograph in this series, the mounted troops are United States Marines in Santo Domingo (4.20); their power is accentuated not only by their physical presence and the fog-enshrouded atmosphere of the day, but also by the *absence* of other human figures, except for the solitary small girl in a corner building doorway. In 4.21 we see a tiny, dark soldier, almost smaller in height than his rifle. Finally, two rare photographs by an anonymous photographer using a box camera show Union soldiers liberating General Wyler's concentration camp in Cuba in 1898 (4.22 and 4.23).

4.18 Indian woman before troops, HH

4.19 Parading troops in Mexico City, CMP

4.20 U.S. Marines in Santo Domingo, BV
4.21 Tiny soldier, AM

4.22 Emaciated prisoners, Cuba, RF   4.23 Soldiers liberating camp, Cuba, RF

Native People (I)
Two portraits, circa 1880, of Indian warriors taken during Ferrez's trip to the interior use so carelessly erected backdrops that the photographer's undraped equipment stands in the way (4.24a and 4.24b). The public wanted views of warlike Indians, and Ferrez obliged.

Four young Indian women in the Ichuantepec Isthmus of Mexico are posed in a "natural" tropical setting (4.25). Two, carrying objects on their heads, stand facing one another for no apparent purpose. A third sits dolefully with her legs apart, the position of her toes showing the strain of holding the pose for a long time; and a fourth lies prone in a coquettish manner. The cameraman was not trying to capture women in the act of work; he considered them to be exotic and primitive. This supposedly artistic approach to photographing them strips them of dignity, making them objects of curiosity.

Native People (II)
Even these shots taken in a natural setting depended on the photographer and on the willingness of his subjects. The subjects of a photo-

4.24a and b Ferrez, Posed Indians, GF

graph of a family group sitting in a long dugout canoe (probably taken near the Bolivian-Brazilian border) show a range of reactions (4.26): the man near the center looks down and away, and the elderly figure next to him sits angrily, covered by a blanket. Some of the others show sullen faces, or polite stares; no one seems obviously happy.

In a portrait taken during the 1879–80 Conquest of the Desert campaign, Argentine soldiers and priests shepherd a group of several dozen Indian boys, all dressed in military uniforms (4.27). They are being baptized en masse. Were they also impressed into military service? In 4.28 Patagonian Indians sit in front of a shelter constructed of animal skins. They seem stunned; no attempt has been made to calm them or to regroup them to please the lens.

4.25 Native girls of Ichuantepec, CMP

4.27 Conquest of the Desert campaign, EW

4.26 Indians in canoe, HH

4.28 Patagonian Indians, EW

Children (I)

Children of the elite were portrayed as little aristocrats, as indeed they were. Nineteenth-century photographers posed them in adultlike ways, attributing to them a sense of solemnity or precocity. In 4.29, a photograph taken in the mid-1850s, a boy poses with a black slave nanny. She sits erectly, protecting her charge behind her ample brocaded skirt. Her greying hair hints at long and honored service to the family. The boy is affectionate to her, even if he tries hard to be a "little man."

The young girls in 4.30 are participating in a civic pageant; they represent the nine Colombian states in 1872. The allegory is authentically choreographed to the extent that a genuine carriage and two male footmen are provided. Dressed in white with bridelike veils, the girls appear innocent and very much protected from the real world.

The two child beggars in 4.31 and 4.32 exemplify the way elites wanted to see the children of the poor; they are ragged but not malnourished. One of them seems good-humored, even mischievous. One faintly evokes sympathy; the other does not. There is such a significant dif-ference between the way that both of these children were posed and the way that cameramen typically photographed children in institutions that it is tempting to guess that there was more sympathy for urchins that roamed the street than for youths in the care of the state. Compare the beggars in 4.31 and 4.32 to the woeful school children in 3.14b, who were scrutinized with such sharpness of focus and so dwarfed by their desks that all compassion is drained from the image. Even the photographer's rich use of shadow in 4.32 adds an element of humanity, which is totally lacking from the orphan school portrait.

4.29 Boy and nanny, BK

4.30 Colombian civic pageant, ES

4.31 Beggar, HH
4.32 Beggar, HH

4.33 Ecuadorean shopping arcade, HH

4.34 Chambi, Cuzcan mother and child, MC

Children (II)

The children in the photograph of an Ecuadorean shopping arcade (4.33; which includes, in the background, a photographer's studio) are accidental, in the sense that the main subjects were the derby-hatted shopkeeper and the well-dressed small child at his side. The children who are seated (one stands with a box on his head), waiting to be hired as porters, were clearly secondary in importance as far as the photographer was concerned. What we have is a glimpse of two worlds coexisting side by side.

Chambi's portrait of a Cuzcan mother and child is contrived (4.34): the woman holds her spinning bobbin in a rather useless way, and she is obviously posed against a studio backdrop. But they seem real enough. She is barefoot but dignified; the child is patient and protected. On the whole, studio photographs of children sometimes offer more insight than photographs of adults, because children were "not encouraged to efface themselves into a timeless pose."[7]

4.35 Wedding couple, Goiás, AM

4.36a Wedding couple, Guatemala, TU

4.36b Wedding couple, Mexico, TU

Weddings (I)

The bride and bridegroom of 4.35, a working-class couple from the interior state of Goiás in Brazil, are stereotyped by their clothing (she wears a simple white dress; both carry umbrellas, to protect against the sun) and by the unnatural angle of the camera. Two other images (one from Guatemala, the other from Mexico) follow the timeless conventions of wedding portraiture that were applied throughout the region (4.36a and 4.36b). The setting is ornate, the couple formally dressed. The bridegroom is seated and the bride stands over him, dominat-

ing the scene, in fact. This was probably done in order to show her gown.

Weddings (II)

More natural is the wedding photograph of 4.37: a Lebanese-Brazilian couple from Guaratinguetá in the state of São Paulo. The picture was copied from a family album. She poses elegantly in her gown, holding flowers; he stands handsomely in his military uniform. Their arms curve down their sides in exactly the same manner, lending an air of symmetry to the image.

Chambi's photograph of the Gadea wedding party in Cuzco demonstrates his uncanny ability to capture deeper layers of meaning in conventional subjects (4.38). The lovely bride holds a wilting bouquet; her husband, in Max Kozloff's words, "looks like a worried mortician."[8] The wedding party is dreamlike and surreal.

4.38 Chambi, Gadea wedding, MC

4.37 Lebanese-Brazilian couple, JLS

4.39 Gauchos, HH

4.40a Contractors engineers, HH

4.40b Villahermosa agricultural trainees, SHSW

Work (I)

In 4.39 gauchos are posed in front of hundreds of drying hides, suggesting hard work but also prosperity and plenty. The group portrait of the "Contractors Engineers" at the Buenos Aires Harbor Works shows eight dapper young men, all English, with arms crossed jauntily or hands thrust into the pockets of striped trousers (4.40a). A group of Mexican agricultural trainees in an orphan school in Villahermosa, Tabasco, are photographed dramatically in near silhouette (4.40b). The scene bursts with energy—nowhere suggesting toil. Certainly, not one of these three "portraits" conveys the reality of these jobs.

4.41 Mexican water carriers, HH

4.42 Paraguayan maté carriers, HH

4.43a Pottery vendors, SHSW

Work (II)

In viewing 4.41, our eyes are drawn immediately to the cruel weight curving the backs of the Mexican water carriers, to their shoeless feet, and to their raggedness. The first man may be a Chinese coolie. They apparently have just filled their containers and are setting out on their arduous rounds. In the case of the Paraguayan maté carriers, their sacks are so bulky and enveloping that we see nothing at all of the face and upper torso of the peasant on the right (4.42). The Mexican pottery vendors, some of them boys, carry ranks of clay pots which must easily exceed one hundred pounds in (4.43a). They stand bowed by the weight and wear nothing on their feet but flat sandals. A

4.43b Human taxi, HH

few sets of eyes show exhaustion or despair; yet their work day has apparently just begun. Another image captures a human taxi—a man transporting a passenger on his back (4.43b). This practice was common not only in Mexico, where the photograph was taken, but in the Andean countries also, well into the early twentieth century.

The problem with using these harsh images to generalize is that as documentation they are fragmentary and incomplete. For instance, we do not know whether other carriers bore lighter or heavier burdens. Perhaps those performing the cruelest tasks were singled out because such images would sell better to armchair tourists or collectors of the exotic. Still, though it is difficult to draw conclusions about whole societies from these images, they do offer a counterpoint to the idealized posed images that were manufactured to convey the dignity of work under a dominant, benevolent gaze.

Urban Life (I)

Early cityscapes were relatively empty and devoid of movement, as in this view of Recife's Rua Cadeia Nova, because cameras could not capture motion (4.44). Photographs of city streets after the 1860s boasted of construction and civic accomplishment. The Ferrez photograph of Rio de Janeiro's Avenida Central in 1906 starkly isolates the new office building so that the viewer can examine its detail without distraction (4.45). The picture is so devoid of life that the tiny trees and lamps on the street appear to be dollhouse figures. The men on the sidewalk next to Montevideo's Bank of the River Plate seem equally dwarfed by the massive granite structure which fills the photograph with sweeping diagonal lines to the horizon (4.46).

4.44 Recife, Rua Cadeia Nova, GF

4.45 Avenida Central, Rio de Janeiro, GF

4.46 Bank of River Plate, HH

4.47 Duperly, Corpus Christi procession, Bogotá, ES

4.48 Woman on balcony, Quito, HH

Urban Life (II)

Henri Duperly's photograph of Bogotá's Calle Real during the Corpus Christi procession in 1895 offers not only unusual detail—some penitents are marching on their knees—but also a view, on a grand scale, of a functioning city, its sidewalks twenty-deep with onlookers, its balconies packed (4.47). The procession emanates from the cathedral and winds out as the street widens.

That Latin American cities were congested, noisy, foul smelling, and piled with heaps of garbage comes through in few surviving photographs. The photograph of a young woman standing on a hotel balcony overlooking Quito's Calle Bolívar offers a believable sense of city life without masking its texture (4.48).

Rural Life (I)

Consider the static, almost formal photograph of an oxcart standing motionless in a Venezuelan pasture (4.49). Children pose dutifully in the wagon; another boy blocks the oxen from the front, and a frocked priest stands at the side, as if to bless the scene. The countryside is

4.49 Venezuelan oxcart, CMP
4.50 Cuban plantation scene, HH

orderly, its boundaries marked in part by a fence of logs. The figures are posed low enough below the horizon to accentuate the billowing clouds, which romanticize the image. The composition lacks emotional space; the figures do not touch or relate to each other. A frontal perspective anchors the oxcart, the beasts of burden, and the priest to the earth. This photograph is barren although it was presumably made to suggest plenty. The Cuban 1855 harvest scene shows oxcarts piled high with sugarcane (4.50). A man or woman stands on each cart as if guarding the harvest. Only one figure is actually bending and working. The draught animals are resting; and the man on horseback—probably an overseer, possibly carrying a whip in his hand—looks away, without interest. The image conveyed, then, is of plenty, labor docility, and relative effortlessness (note the woman standing on the high wheel of the nearest cart). But unanswered questions remain: Why are most of the workers women? Did the photographer deliberately wait until the field labor was completed? Will the remaining stalks be picked up or left on the ground?

Rural Life (II)

The Mexican sugarcane harvesters of 4.51 contrast distinctly with the previous image. The setting is virtually identical, but the photographer, rather than interrupt the cutters, shows them at work. The feeling of backbreaking labor is accentuated by the blurs caused by movement of arms and legs. The piled cane almost dwarfs the men, who toil under the eye of a man on horseback who faces them directly (the overseer in the posed photograph was looking away).

A Cuban family at the turn of the century stands outside their thatched-roof hut in 4.52. The adults are well enough dressed, but the naked children show signs of malnourishment —primarily distended stomachs. One of the boys wears a pair of shoes; the other, like the infants, is shoeless. (In tropical environments lack of shoes commonly leads to parasitic disease.)

The Mexican washerwomen of 4.53 are using stone basins in a municipal facility alongside a river; they are so hard at work that they do not look at the camera. A wide-angle photograph of peons hoping to be called for day labor at a

4.51 Mexican cane harvest, CMP

sugar refinery in Tamasofo, Mexico, captures the anxious life of the rural wage worker (4.54). The laborers stand in clumps, their serapes wrapped around them for warmth; they are at the mercy of an exploitive system.

A biwinged seaplane lands amidst a huddled group of Highland Indians: the gleaming, reflected light on the airplane contrasts with the dark and somber human figures in this photograph by Sebastian Rodriguez (4.55). It is as if a magical bird from the twentieth century has momentarily visited the nineteenth-century lives of the isolated mountain residents. What we know about the actual event, however, illustrates the hazards of attempting analysis from the photograph alone. In reality the hydroplane ran out of fuel and was forced to land on the highland lake. The townspeople were so awed by this visitation that they clamored to have their pictures taken, and Rodriguez dutifully set up his camera in the right spot. People arrived "in droves" to be photographed in front of the airplane.[9]

4.52 Rural Cuban family, RF

4.53 Mexican washerwomen, CMP

4.54 Day laborers, SHSW

4.55 Rodriguez, Biplane, FA

Ethnicity

Not unlike the United States and Canada, Latin America received tens of thousands of immigrants from all over the world in the nineteenth and early twentieth centuries. The fact that immigrants came from Asia, the Middle East, North Africa, and Southern and Eastern Europe is not entirely evident from most written histories, which tend to emphasize the descendants of the Spanish and Portuguese. Photographs reveal the variety of the ethnic mix. Here are two photographs of circus performers, one a Japanese family who traveled throughout South America before settling in Brazil (4.56); the other is of a troupe of Spaniards emigrating to Mexico (4.57). The visa photograph is of Pasqualina Scinocca, an Italian emigrant to Brazil during the period when planters in the south attempted to substitute agricultural colonists from Europe for slaves (4.58). The Yucatecan baseball player is a member of Mérida's "Cuba" team, reminding us of the movement of both culture and population within the Caribbean basin before the First World War (4.59).

4.56 Japanese circus family, BK

4.58 Pasqualina Scinocca visa
photograph, BK

4.59 Baseball player, GJ

4.57 Spanish circus group in Mexico, CMP

4.60 Havana's municipal theater, HH
4.61 Teatro São José, São Paulo, HH

Leisure (I)

A photograph of Havana's Municipal Theater (1898), taken for a stereoscopic travelogue, shows an empty stage and audience (4.60). Twenty-two years later a photograph of São Paulo's grand Teatro São José shows only empty chairs on the stage and not a soul in the audience (4.61). This was not the point. The municipal authorities who paid for such photographs wanted to show off the ornate furnishings and the solid construction of the theaters. The theaters are remarkably similar and are more European than Latin American in style. The Havana Theater's dome is decorated with cherubim and angels; the interior of the Teatro São José is dominated by a frieze of similar figures and is bounded on each side by larger-than-life paintings of women seductively posed in the classical fashion associated with high culture in eighteenth- and nineteenth-century Europe. To the clients who paid for these photographs, it was more important to show these details than to have a full house for the photographer's lens.

Chambi's 1928 photograph of the German technical staff at the *Cervecería Cusco* depicts somber, stiff, well-groomed men with little feel-

ing of genuine leisure or relaxation (4.62). Each man smokes a cigarette while he holds his glass of beer. Could the men have felt awkward in the presence of the photographer, with his Indian features and primitive camera? Chambi's composition of Cuscan dignitaries walking in parade fashion through local streets sharply contrasts the ceremonial and formal ways of the elite (there are several kinds of uniforms in the photograph, and even the women's elegant finery seems to be a kind of uniform) against the solitary image of a black-cloaked peasant woman walking toward them (4.63).

Leisure (II)

Spontaneity is more difficult to capture. This rare photograph of Brazilian Carnival, taken in 1898 in the forested, mountainous interior of the state of Minas Gerais, shows the festival's quasi-religious aspects (4.64). Celebrants gather on horseback, some in conical hats reminiscent of ceremonial church garb; others carry banners of the type carried in religious processions. The elevated vantage point of the camera adds to the sense of candidness—as if the pho-

4.62 Chambi, German brewery technicians, MC

4.63 Chambi, Cuzcan dignitaries in procession, MC

4.64 Early Brazilian Carnival, HH

tographer captured the town's residents at a moment of ease.

Chambi's depiction of Carnival celebrants in a small room differs from most evocations of revelry because his subjects seem to be more festive than self-conscious (4.65): the man in the skeleton suit looks like he has a stomach-ache; the woman at top center is trying to be tipsy. Some of the party goers have dusted white powder on their faces, perhaps a holdover of the medieval carnival custom of white masks. Similarly, the photograph of celebrants of the *Guardia Civil* in Sascayhuaman overflows with human interest in small vignettes (4.66). Some of the men hold guitars, as if the closeness of the scene would permit them to play. Most of the uniformed policemen seem aggressively proud of themselves: one holds a glass of beer; several smoke cigars. An older officer holds his arm around a younger man, as if he were a sweetheart. Family members within the main body of the photograph seem relaxed; on the periphery cling small boys and at least one adult peasant, some ragged and barefoot, who apparently wandered into the picture. Chambi's decision to cram all of his subjects into the crevice

4.65 Chambi, Carnival celebrants, MC

4.66 Chambi, Guardia civil, MC

4.67 Chambi, Butcher's Association, MC

of an overgrown Incan wall lends another level of imagery to this composition posed near the site of Macchu Picchu.

The speaker from the Butcher's Association addressed a more subdued audience in 4.67. The men's hats are in their hands. Behind the table sit family members (of the hacienda?) and the officers of the association, the men smug, the woman seemingly apprehensive. Younger men and boys (apprentices?) line the low fence behind the speaker's table. His stance, his suit, and his manner remind us of Buster Keaton; but everyone else stares solemnly, if not glumly, ahead.

A final Chambi photograph, of a religious festival among Indian peasants, contrasts the wan celebrants with the large and elegantly dressed upper-class group looking down at them from the hacienda's balcony (4.68). The social distance between the two levels is stunning.

Two photographs depict groups of street musicians. One, from Minas Gerais in 1875, shows a group made up entirely of blacks, except for the young cornet player in the front (4.69); a bearded white man holds up a white flag as if

4.68 Chambi, Religious festival, MC

to assure the camera of his group's friendliness. A less organized band of youths stands at the entrance to the Teatro Colon in Sánchez, the Dominican Republic (4.70). The clarinet player is sharply dressed in a striped suit and a hat; the others are barefoot. The double feature playing is serious enough: "The Last Days of Pompeii" and "Notre Dame de Paris." The sign reminds the viewer that a sharp two-class system divided the population; it is unlikely that any of the shoeless boys would have the opportunity to view such films.

Who took the accidental and less-posed photographs in the second sets of images reproduced here? In some cases, the same photographers who manufactured the traditional kinds of depictions in the first set. Far fewer of the less-posed photographs survive, since they were not nearly as commercially lucrative. In fact, in collections and archives images of the first sort outnumber those of the second perhaps in a ratio of forty or fifty to one. Obviously the early photographers were first and foremost businessmen and could not afford to take pictures which could not be sold. But some con-

4.69 Street musicians, Minas Gerais, GF

sumers must have preferred to see life nearer to what it really was like. Still, only after the start of the twentieth century (and in most cases considerably later) did photographers in Latin America begin to produce, with any frequency, compositions that could be considered unflattering or bluntly realistic.

Photographs unfailingly reflect the values and priorities of the photographer and society at large. If photographs reduce truth to fact, as critics argue, then these facts are potentially documents to serve as the basis for historical analysis. All varieties of photographs are inherently valuable. Contrived poses to some degree must reveal the mind of the cameraman; random or accidental images help correct interpretive disparities and add further dimensions to the world of images.

Posed photographs, of course, are invested with the routine deception created when, in the extreme, the "psychological slack has been pulled taut to assert the prepared, immobile display" of the subject by the photographer.[10] Knowing this permits a closer understanding of the motives and outlook of the photographer, since the very standardization of posing (light-

4.70 Street musicians, BV

ing, backgrounds, posing conventions) permits us to draw conclusions, if we have many works by the same photographer for comparison.

Even so, some claim that we are left with a feeling that beyond the variant pictorial codes of the images "lies something that defeats understanding."[11] This is less valid for the social historian than it is for the photo historian, who is more interested in critical interpretation of the image and the techniques that produced it than in larger linkages to society and social mores. Photographs are time bound, yet possess contemporary relevance. Their medium is temporal as well as spatial. When we use photographs as documents we acknowledge the assumption that believable history involves an imaginative ordering of materials in the pursuit of recreating experience.[12] Photographs are all the more useful when we understand that photographers select and shape images to formulate unifying myths in the service of evolving societies.

Photographs can yield contextual data if analyzed in a disciplined way; but one must never forget that photographs say many different things and that we tend to see what we are predisposed to see, however "scientific" our intent. Comparison of images is very helpful when it is possible, and it reduces the chance that strong conclusions will result from isolated likenesses. It may be accurate to say that much photographic work represents collusion between photographer and subject, or intimidation by the photographer mixed with social pressure. Understanding the social context in which a photograph was taken, then, helps lessen the risks involved in attempting to extract meaningful information from that image.

Notes

Introduction

1. Gilberto Freyre, *O escravo nos anúncios de jornais brasileiros do século XIX*.

2. Anita Brenner, *The Wind that Swept Mexico: the History of the Mexican Revolution, 1910–1942*; Gustavo Casasola, *História gráfica de la Revolución Mexicana, 1900–1960*, an expanded version of Agustín V. Casasola's 1921 *Album histórico gráfico*.

3. Paul J. Vanderwood and Frank N. Samponaro, *A Picture Postcard Record of Mexico's Revolution and U.S. War Preparedness, 1910–1917* (Albuquerque: University of New Mexico Press, 1988).

4. "Reciprocal Influence," *Princeton Alumni Weekly*, p. 16.

5. John Collier, "Visual Anthropology," in Jon Wagner, ed., *Images of Information*, p. 271. See Edward T. Hall, *The Hidden Dimension*, on the use of space in anthropological research, and Ray L. Birdwhistell, *Kinesics and Context*.

6. Bryan Brown, ed., *The England of Henry Taunt, Victorian Photographer*, Introduction.

7. See Julia Hirsch, *Family Photographs: Content, Meaning, and Effect*, p. 44.

8. Michael Lesy, "The Photography of History," p. 2.

9. William H. McNeill, *Mythistory and Other Essays*, p. 4.

10. James West Davidson and Mark Hamilton Lytle, *After the Fact: the Art of Historical Detection*, pp. 221–22.

11. Pedro Vasquez, "Olha o'passarinho'!," in Gilberto Freyre, *O Retrato Brasileiro*, p. 31.

12. Susan Sontag, *On Photography*, pp. 5–6.

13. Eugen Weber, *Peasants into Frenchmen: the Modernization of Rural France, 1870–1914*, p. 231.

14. See Gilberto Freyre, *Vida social no Brasil nos meados do século XIX*. (Originally published in English in 1922 in the *Hispanic American Historical Review* 5:597–630.)

15. Collier, "Visual Anthropology," p. 277.

16. See Robert U. Atkeret, *Photoanalysis*, pp. 32–33.

17. Lesy, "The Photography of History," 3.

18. Kathleen Logan, "Arches and Transitions: A Photographic Essay of Mérida, Yucatán, México," in Robert M. Levine, ed., *Windows on Latin America* (Coral Gables: SECOLAS, 1987), p. 116.

1   The Daguerreotype Era

1. See Marc Ferro, *The Use and Abuse of History*, p. 237.

2. For an overview of the early years of the Hispanic New World empires, see Lyle N. McAlister, *Spain and Portugal in the New World, 1492–1700*, especially pp. 455–459.

3. See Eugene W. Ridings, "Foreign Predominance among Overseas Traders in Nineteenth-Century Latin America," pp. 3–28.

4. Thomas E. Skidmore and Peter H. Smith, *Modern Latin America*, pp. 41, 39–42.

5. Nancy Stepan, *Beginnings of Brazilian Science*, pp. 16–23.

6. Michel F. Braive, *The Photograph: A Social History*, p. 55.

7. Susan Sontag, *On Photography*, p. 23.

8. Peter Galassi, *Before Photography: Painting and the Invention of Photography*, p. 12.

9. Beaumont Newhall, *The History of Photography from 1839 to Present*, pp. 11–14; Oliver Mathews, *Early Photographs and Early Photographers* (New York: Pittman Publishing Corp., 1973), pp. 1–2. For discussion of the invention of photography in a social context, see also Walter Benjamin, "A Short History of Photography," pp. 46–51; Gisèle Freund, *La Photographie en France au dixneuvième siècle*; and Richard Rudisill, *Mirror Image: The Influence of the Daguerreotype on American Society*.

10. Some historians argue that Bayard should be given credit for the invention of photography, since he was the first to produce and exhibit positive paper prints. See Robert Sobieszek, "Historical Commentary," citing Georges Pontoniée, *The History of the Discovery of Photography*, translated by Edward Epstean (New York: Tennant and Ward, 1936), p. 186.

11. The main reason was that Florence did not seem to realize the significance of his discovery. See Robert A. Sobieszek, Introduction to "Hercules Florence, Pioneer of Photography in Brazil," by Boris Kossoy. See also Weston J. Naef, "Hercules Florence, 'Inventor do Photografia',"; Alfredo Santos Pressacco, "Hercules Florence, primeiro fotógrafo de América?"

12. Hercules Florence, *Livre d'annotations et des primiers materiaux*, cited by Kossoy, "Hercules Florence," p. 16.

13. Pedro Vasquez, *Dom Pedro II e a Fotografia no Brasil*, pp. 19–20; Robert A. Sobieszek, Introduction to Boris Kossoy, "Hercules Florence." See also Boris Kossoy, *Hercules Florence. 1833: A descoberta isolada da fotografia no Brasil*. As Peter Galassi has pointed out, the curious thing about the invention of photography was that although the men who were working so feverishly to perfect the process seem to have been in a race, none knew about the work of any of the others. Even the label of "discoverer" depends on what characteristic of the early medium is taken to have been the most significant. But the fact remains that Florence is almost always omitted from the lists of the early inventors. See *Before Photography: Painting and the Invention of Photography* (New York: Museum of Modern Art, 1981), pp. 12–13.

14. Sobieszek, "Historical Commentary."

15. Sontag, *On Photography*, p. 63.

16. Ridings, "Foreign Predominance among Overseas Traders," p. 16.

17. Beaumont Newhall, *The Daguerreotype in America*, p. 79.

18. See Bryan Brown, ed., *The England of Henry Taunt, Victorian Photographer,* Introduction. For an impressive example of the detail captured by naturalistic artists in the early nineteenth century, see João Maurício Rugendas, *Viagem pitoresca através do Brasil.*

19. Newhall, *The Daguerreotype in America*, pp. 22–23, citing Seager's booklet, *The Resources of Mexico apart from the Precious Metals* (Mexico City: J. White, 1867).

20. Ian Jeffrey, *Photography: A Concise History*, p. 10; Keith McElroy, *Early Peruvian Photography: A Critical Case Study*, p. 2; H. L. Hoffenberg, *Nineteenth-Century South America in Photographs.*

21. See Instituto Autonomo Biblioteca Nacional y de Servicios de Bibliotecas, *Orígenes de la fotografía en Venezuela*, p. 1. Daguerre's manual went through 21 editions in two years and was translated into every major language.

22. In 1852 the Russian Consul-General presented him with a large box of camera equipment. Throughout his reign foreign governments and diplomats gave Pedro collections of photographs, presentation albums, books, and assorted equipment. See Vasquez, *Dom Pedro II*, p. 28.

23. Ricardo Martim [Guilherme Auler], "Dom Pedro e a fotografia," cited by Gilberto Ferrez, *A fotografia no Brasil, 1840–1900*, p. 20. See also McElroy, *Early Peruvian Photography*, p. 3. The story of Compte's visit to South America is provided in José Maria Fernandez Saldana, "La Fotografia en el Rio de la Plata," and in Amado Becquer Casaballe and Miguel Angel Cuarterolo, *Cronica de la fotografia rioplatense, 1840–1940*, pp. 12–16.

24. Prior to 1842 no photograph could have recorded the amount of motion captured by Morand's camera. See Gilberto Ferrez and Weston J. Naef, *Pioneer Photographers of Brazil: 1840–1920*, pp. 16–17. See also Casaballe and Cuarterolo, *Cronica*, pp. 13–14.

25. Newhall, *The Daguerreotype in America*, p. 11.

26. International Center of Photography, *ICP Encyclopedia of Photography*, pp. 130–31.

27. *Cartas de Alvares de Azevedo* (São Paulo: Academia Paulista de Letras, 1976), p. 76, quoting from Manoel Antonio Alvares de Azevedo. Cited by Boris Kossoy, "Militão Augusto de Azevedo of Brazil: The Photographic Documentation of São Paulo (1862–1887)," p. 9.

28. Germán Rodrigo Mejía, "Colombian Photographs of the Nineteenth and Early Twentieth Centuries," p. 58.

29. Elizabeth Heyert, *The Glass House Years: Victorian Portrait Photography, 1839–1870*, p. 3. Beard's studio was the only one in London until several opened in 1847–48.

30. Ferrez and Naef, *Pioneer Photographers of Brazil*, p. 17, citing Beaumont Newhall, *Latent Image: the Discovery of Photography* (Garden City: Doubleday, 1967), pp. 72–73, and *Relatorio apresentado ao Governo pela comissão diretora da Exposição de Pernambuco de 1866* (Recife, n.d.). Aguiles Nazor, *Caracas fisica y espiritual* (Caracas: Litografia Tecnocolor, 1977), p. 94; Casaballe and Cuarterolo, *Cronica*, pp. 19–20.

31. Newhall, *The Daguerreotype in America*, pp. 72–73; William Welling, *Photography in America. The Formative Years 1839–1900*, p. 358.

32. *Anthony's Photographic Bulletin* 12 (1881):110–12, cited by Newhall, *The Daguerreotype in America*, p. 73.

33. Newhall, *The Daguerreotype in America*, p. 73. Newhall says the animal was a "tiger," but unless it had been imported from abroad it was probably a puma or jaguar.

34. Until 1987 it was widely believed that none of Fredricks's South American works had survived. In that year a collection of twelve daguerreotypes, some with

matts embossed "Electrotypo Fredricks e Weeks" (sic.), was offered for sale in New York by a rare book dealer. Priced at $42,000 and dated from the mid-1840s, they include scenes of a black woman and child and a portrait of two small girls. They were taken in the north of Brazil, probably Recife. See Richard C. Ramer, "Daguerreo-types," p. 32. See also Lisa Bloom, "Charles De Forest Fredricks: 19th Century Entrepreneur in the Photography Industry."

35. International Center of Photography, *Encyclopedia*, p. 403.

36. Eugenio S. Pereira, "El centenario de la fotografía en Chile, 1840–1940."

37. Vasquez, *Dom Pedro II*, p. 23.

38. See Ferrez and Naef, *Pioneer Photographers of Brazil*, p. 32, note 6. The documented amount, totaling 18,796 mil-réis over twenty years, seems improbably high, but histori-ans have not challenged the figures.

39. Pedro Vasquez, "Brazilian Photography in the Nine-teenth Century."

40. See figure 1.7 above for an example of Bennet's work.

41. Eduardo Serrano, *Historia de la fotografía en Colombia*, pp. 41–44.

42. *El Comercio* (Lima), 26 March 1856, quoted by McElroy, *Early Peruvian Photography*, p. 5.

43. Newhall, *The Daguerreotype in America*, p. 35.

44. Gisèle Freund, *Photography & Society*, pp. 28–33.

45. See Heyert, *The Glass House Years*, p. 58.

46. International Center of Photography, *Encyclopedia*, p. 404.

47. Serrano, *Historia de la fotografía*, pp. 36–37.

48. "Daguerreotipo," *El Comercio* (Lima), 8 July 1842, p. 4.

49. Jed Perl, "Japan: Photographs, 1854–1905," p. 36. Commodore Perry brought a daguerreotypist with him in 1853, but the images were destroyed in a fire later.

2 Order and Progress

1. Keith McElroy, *Early Peruvian Photography: A Critical Case Study*, p. xvii.

2. See Gilberto Ferrez and Weston J. Naef, *Pioneer Photog-raphers of Brazil: 1840–1920*, p. 22.

3. Robert Sobieszek, "Historical Commentary."

4. Margaret Loke, "Frozen in Time," p. 48.

5. Gisèle Freund, *Photography and Society*, pp. 53–58.

6. Elizabeth Heyert, *The Glass-House Years: Victorian Por-trait Photography, 1839–1870*, p. 83.

7. International Center of Photography, *Encyclopedia*, "carte de visite," p. 99. In the United States Abraham Lincoln attributed his first election to his Cooper Union speech and to *cartes* made and distributed by the thou-sands by Matthew Brady in New York and another pho-tographer in Chicago.

8. One example of such an album is stored in the Special Collections of the University of New Mexico, Zimmer-man Library, Box 12.5.

9. Cited by Glen E. Holt, "Chicago Through a Camera Lens: An Essay on Photography as History," p. 160.

10. McElroy, *Early Peruvian Photography*, p. 21, citing *El Comercio*, 18 July 1859, p. 3.

11. As far as we know, photographs of slaves were *not* used in the cause of abolition, as they were in the United States, where abolitionists coveted *cartes* of slave children who looked white to shock audiences. See Kathleen Col-lins, "Portraits of Slave Children."

12. Ferrez and Naef, *Pioneer Photographers of Brazil*, p. 64.

13. International Center of Photography, *Encyclopedia*, "cabinet photograph," p. 89.

14. Ferrez and Naef, *Pioneer Photographers of Brazil*, p. 93.

15. Elizabeth Anne McCauley, *A.A.E. Disdéri and the Carte-de-Visite Photograph*, p. 3

16. See, for example, W. H. Fox Talbot, *The Pencil of Nature; Sun Pictures in Scotland* (1845); Peter H. Emerson, *Life and Landscape of the Norfolk Broads* (1886); *Pictures of East Anglian Life* (1888).

17. McElroy, *Early Peruvian Photography*, p. 25.

18. See McCauley, *A. A. E. Disdéri*, Ch. 3; Amado Becquer Casaballe and Miguel Angel Cuarterolo, *Crónica de la fotografía rioplatense, 1840–1940*, p. 29.

19. "Retratos," *El Comercio* (Lima), 31 May 1852, p. 3, and Fuentes's proposal to the government, dated 12 August 1858, cited in McElroy, *Early Peruvian Photography*, p. 11.

20. H. L. Hoffenberg, *Nineteenth-Century South America in Photographs*, p. 42. One "poster" contained portraits of foreign-born wanted men; the other Uruguayans.

21. See Sobieszek, "Historical Commentary."

22. "Nueva aplicación del daguerrotipo," *El Comercio,* 14 March 1840, p. 2, cited in McElroy, *Early Peruvian Photography,* p. 3. Given the daguerreotype camera's need for lengthy exposures, the lover must have dallied considerably at the window if the newspaper account is to be believed.

23. Fox Talbot, *Pencil of Nature,* cited by Ian Jeffrey, *Photography: A Concise History,* p. 12.

24. For example, his painting of Notre Dame Cathedral in the late 1830s, with the massive structure in silhouette overshadowing "idlers" and street people. See Jeffrey, *Photography,* p. 16.

25. See Richard M. Morse, "Claims of Political Tradition," pp. 420–21, quoting Kenneth Burke (no source given). Ironically, African and Amerindian culture persisted to a much greater degree in Catholic Central and South America than in Protestant North America, and in the nineteenth century the Latin American elite rejected socially Catholic Iberia.

26. Peter Bacon Hales, *Silver Cities: the Photography of American Urbanization, 1839–1915,* p. 11.

27. See *El Federalist* (Caracas), 29 Oct. 1858, p. 1.

28. Humberto Cuenca, *Imagen literaria del periodismo,* p. 191. See also Josune Dorronsoro, *Significación histórica de la fotografía.*

29. The official, Lélis Piedade, a journalist and war correspondent, was quite well known in the region for his work with the survivors and his face was probably more recognizable than the governor's. A photograph of the Lampião safe-conduct photographic card is reprinted in Rui Facó, *Cangaceiros e Fanáticos,* 5th ed. (Rio de Janeiro: Civilização Brasileira, 1978), p. 17.

30. Susan Sontag, *On Photography,* p. 23.

31. Except for Fredricks's photographs of Cuba taken between 1855 and 1857, we know of only about two dozen outdoor photographs in the hemisphere, mostly in Cuba and Venezuela. Fredricks himself was one of the first daguerreotypists to shoot outdoors, in the 1840s, when he produced views of buildings in Buenos Aires and in Recife. Only a few sets of pre-Civil War photographs (of North American sites) are known to have survived to our day. Early outdoor views, whether daguerreotypes or photographs made with newer processes, are extremely rare.

32. See, for example, Carlos E. Pellegrini's "El negro Biguá" (1841), a depiction of a retarded black street clown who performed for alms in the streets of Rosas's Buenos Aires (Bonifacio del Carril and Aníbal G. Aguirre Saravia, *Iconografía de Buenos Aires: La ciudad de Garay hasta 1852,* p. 194).

33. Eduardo Serrano, *Historia de la fotografía en Colombia,* p. 146.

34. Ferrez and Naef, *Pioneer Photographers,* pp. 23–24.

35. Ferrez and Naef, *Pioneer Photographers,* p. 114.

36. See Boris Kossoy, *Origens e expansão da fotografia no Brasil: século xix,* pp. 54–76; Boris Kossoy, "Militão Augusto de Azevedo of Brazil."

37. Kossoy, *Origens,* p. 12, citing A. E. Zaluar, *Peregrinação pela provincia de São Paulo (1860–61),* p. 136.

38. The power of the client to demand poses falling within prescribed convention arguably increased greatly with the availability of proof sets, from which customers chose. Daguerreotype subjects had to accept the single image presented to them.

39. McElroy, *Early Peruvian Photography,* p. 17.

40. McElroy, *Early Peruvian Photography,* p. 64. See "Acuerdo fotografico," *El Mercurio,* 15 Sept. 1863, p. 2; *El Comercio,* 18 Sept. 1863), p. 1, cited by McElroy, *Early Peruvian Photography,* p. 59.

41. McElroy, *Early Peruvian Photography,* pp. 48–49.

42. Paulo Cesar de Azevedo and Mauricio Lissovsky, *Escravos Brasileiros do século xix na fotografia de Christiano Jr.,* p. xii.

43. Obituary in *Caras y Caretas* (Buenos Aires), 13 December 1902.

44. For the history of blacks in photography in the United States, see Pepe Karmel, "Terra Incognita"; Jeanne Moutoussamy-Ashe, *Viewfinders: Black Women Photographers.*

45. See Freund, *Photography & Society,* pp. 66–68; McElroy, *Early Peruvian Photography,* pp. 56–57.

46. See William R. Taylor, "Psyching Out the City," *Uprooted Americans: Essays to Honor Oscar Handlin,* p. 264, on the ways in which Lewis Hine, Jacob Riis, and other reform photographers in the United States may have influenced the way subjects appeared, and even possibly

caused more crowding in small rooms than normal.

47. See Jeffrey, *Photography*, p. 23.

48. McElroy, *Early Peruvian Photography*, pp. 22–29, citing Thomas Hutchinson, *Two Years in Peru*, Vol. I (1873), pp. 321–22.

49. See Julio Philippi Izquierdo, ed., *Vistas de Chile por Rodulfo Amando Philippi*.

50. Edward W. Earle, "Why Photography? Its Place in Our Culture," p. 44.

51. *Atlantic Monthly*, June 1859, p. 744.

52. Earle, "Why Photography?" p. 45.

53. Ferrez and Naef, *Pioneer Photographers*, pp. 24–25.

54. See Benito Panunzi, *Vistas e costumbres de Buenos Aires*.

55. Becquer Casaballe and Cuarterolo, *Crónica*, pp. 40–42.

56. Hales, *Silver Cities*, p. 133.

57. Patricio Gross, Armando de Ramón, and Enrique Vial. *Imágen ambiental de Santiago: 1880–1930*, p. 13.

58. *Caras y Caretas* published a haunting photograph of prisoners from El Chacho (9 Sept. 1899) but without any attribution. The same was true for a photograph of São Paulo's flooded Várzea do Carmo in the great 1902 flood (see *São Paulo: onde está sua história*, plate 284).

59. "No. 2 Francis Thomas to Department of State," Legation of the United States, Lima, 26 July 1872, U.S. Embassy, Peru, *Dispatches from United States Ministers to Peru 1826–1906*, microfilm, T52 roll 24, cited by Keith McElroy, "Montage or Reportage?" p. 232.

60. McElroy, "Montage or Reportage?" p. 232. The photograph, "Bodies of the Gutierrez brothers hanging from the towers of Lima Cathedral," is in the Dammert Collection, Lima.

61. Hales, *Silver Cities*, p. 39; E. Bradford Burns, "Cultures in Conflict: The Implication of Modernization in Nineteenth-Century Latin America," in Virginia Barnhard, ed., *Elites, Masses, and Modernization in Latin America, 1850–1930* (Austin: University of Texas Press, 1979), p. 11.

62. Emília Viotti da Costa, *The Brazilian Empire: Myths and Realities*, p. 171.

63. See Jacob A. Riis, *How the Other Half Lives* (1890; reprint ed., New York: Dover, 1971); Jacob A. Riis, *The Battle with the Slums* (New York: MacMillan, 1902); John Thompson and Adolphe Smith, *Street Life in London*, (appearing in monthly installments from February 1877).

64. Keith McElroy, "La Tapada Limeña: the Iconography of the Veiled Woman in 19th-Century Peru," pp. 133–34, 146.

65. McElroy, "La Tapada Limeña," 146, citing William E. Curtis, *The Capitals of Spanish America* (1888), p. 381.

66. María E. Haya, "Sobre la Fotografía Cubana," *Revolución y Cultura*, no. 93 (1980), p. 45, cited by Ramiro Fernandez, "Cuba: Fotografía 1860–1920, Selected Images from the Collection of Ramiro Fernandez," p. 9.

67. See John A. Kouwenhoven, "The Snapshot." The term "snapshot" was first used by hunters, to mean a "hurried shot taken without deliberate aim."

68. See Kirk Varnedoe, "The Artifice of Candor: Impressionism and Photography Reconsidered," p. 76.

69. See Robert Silberman, "Our Town," esp. p. 104.

70. Paulo Berger, *O Rio de ontem no cartão postal, 1900–1930*.

71. See, for example, *The Republic of Chile: The Growth, Resources, and Industrial Conditions of a Great Nation* (Philadelphia: George Barrie & Sons, 1904); Colonel J. Bascom Jones, ed., *El "Libro Azul" de Guatemala: 1915* (New Orleans: Searcy & Pfaff, 1915).

72. The first illustrated magazines—using drawings and lithographs, not photographs directly—became popular in the 1860s. Rio de Janeiro's *Semana Illustrada* (1860–1976) was the first publication to specialize in cartoon satires of customs and politics. See Boris Kossoy, "Photographic Miscarriage," *History of Photography* 2 (1978): 154. The leading Argentine illustrated magazine was *Caras y Carretas*.

73. An Italian painter, Frederico Trebbi, was contracted by the Brazilian army to photograph the Paraguayan War, but when he arrived he was mostly used to sketch topographic maps, which were used to plan military campaigns. After the war he settled down in Pelotas as a studio photographer. See Pedro Vasquez, "Brazilian Photography in the Nineteenth Century."

74. See Paul J. Vanderwood, "Agustín Casasola in Context," p. 128.

75. See Gustavo Casasola, *História gráfica de la Revolución Mexicana, 1900–1960*.

76. Harvey V. Fondiller, review of "The World of Augustín Víctor Casasola: Mexico, 1900–1938."

77. Eva Cockcroft, "Art and Politics in Latin America"; Vanderwood, "Agustín Casasola in Context," pp. 127–129. Casasola worked for the Mexico City newspaper *El Imparcial*, an eight-page mass circulation daily favorable to the Díaz regime, although reasonably independent.

78. See Ron Tyler, ed., *Posadas Mexico* (Washington, D.C., 1979), cited by Erika Billeter, "Bilder einer Ausstellung," p. 18.

79. See Molly Nesbit, "The Use of History," p. 76, on the impact of the changing photographic marketplace.

80. Max Kozloff, "Chambi of Cuzco," pp. 109–110.

81. See Kozloff, "Chambi of Cuzco," pp. 107–108.

82. See Frances Antmann, "Sebastian Rodriguez's View from Within: The Work of an Andean Photographer in the Mining Town of Morococha, Peru, 1928 to 1968," esp. p. 108. Antmann suggests that Peruvian photography was ultimately adapted to the social and ideological needs of local culture (p. 106). That this occurred in India as well is argued by Judith Mara Gutman, *Through Indian Eyes: 19th and 20th Century Photography from India*.

83. Antmann, "Sebastian Rodriguez's View," p. 106.

84. Commentary by Alberto Flores Galindo, Antonio Cisneros, and Fran Antmann in "The Mining Town of Morococha: Photographs by Sebastian Rodriguez and Fran Antmann," catalog, Museum of Contemporary Hispanic Art, New York, 1986, pp. 1–24.

85. John Tagg, *The Burden of Representation: Essays on Photographies and Histories*, p. 4.

3 Reading Photographs

1. G. Kitson Clark, *Guide for Research Students Working on Historical Subjects*, pp. 30–31; Oscar Handlin, *Truth in History*, pp. 229, 238.

2. Gilberto Ferrez and Weston J. Naef, *Pioneer Photographers of Brazil: 1840–1920*, p. 116.

3. Jacques Barzun and Henry F. Graff, *The Modern Researcher*, p. 147.

4. The role of sugar producers in the regional elite is one of the most exhaustively studied subjects in Brazilian historiography. See the bibliography in Robert M. Levine, *Pernambuco in the Brazilian Federation, 1889–1937* (Stanford: Stanford University Press, 1978).

5. A copy of the photograph was provided by Carlos Bakota; permission to reproduce it was given by Dr. Gilberto Freyre. Details of the photograph were corroborated in conversation by author with Gilberto Freyre, 23 July 1986, Recife.

6. See Germán Rodrigo Mejía, "Colombian Photographs of the Nineteenth and Early Twentieth Centuries," p. 58.

7. Handlin, *Truth in History*, p. 228, citing Richard Henry Dana, *Two Years before the Mast*, (1840; reprint ed., New York, 1909), 61ff., 231.

8. Victor Burgin, *Thinking Photography*, quoted by Halla Beloff, *Camera Culture*, p. 18.

9. My conclusion is based on thorough searching in Salvador's four major archival sources of photographs: the Arquivo Público, the Instituto Geográfico e Histórico, TemPostal, and the Centro de Estudos Baianos of the Universidade Federal da Bahia. On the other hand, we may *want* to read prejudice into images of societies in which we know discrimination occurred although it was officially denied. Who can say what this photograph actually represents?

10. Eugene W. Ridings, "Foreign Predominance among Overseas Traders," p. 17.

11. This is unlikely too, although twentieth-century Cuban and Puerto Rican families sometimes claimed Spanish origin, implying higher social standing.

12. D. F. Eguren de Larrea, *El Cusco, su vida, sus maravillas*.

13. Based on examination of several dozen photographs at the Instituto Geográfico e Histórico in Salvador and at the Fundação Casa Rui Barbosa in Rio de Janeiro, and of contemporary newspapers at these locations and at the Biblioteca Nacional, Rio de Janeiro.

14. Russel B. Nye, "History and Literature," *Essays on History and Literature*, ed. Robert H. Bremner (Columbus: Ohio State University Press, 1966), p. 140.

15. Richard D. Zakia, *Perception and Photography*, pp. 66, 74–75, 77.

16. See Fredric Jameson, *The Political Unconscious* (Ithaca: Cornell University Press, 1981), p. 182.

17. Harold Frederic–Stephen Crane correspondence, in Charles Child Walcutt, *American Naturalism: A Divided*

Stream (Minneapolis: University of Minnesota Press, 1956), p. 89, cited by Carol Shloss, *In Visible Light: Photography and the American Writer, 1840–1940* (New York: Oxford University Press, 1987), p. 17.

18. For a fictional treatment of this theme, see Paul Theroux's *Picture Palace* (New York: Ballantine Books, 1978).

19. Handlin, *Truth in History*, p. 233.

20. Harry Ritter, "Imagination," *Dictionary of Concepts in History*.

21. E. F. im Thurn, "Anthropological Uses of the Camera," p. 78.

22. E. Bradford Burns, *Eadweard Muybridge in Guatemala, 1875. The Photographer as Social Recorder*, p. 3.

23. Robert Bartlett Haas, *Muybridge, Man in Motion*, p. 82.

24. *La Semana*, 14 October 1966, cited in Burns, *Eadweard Muybridge*, p. 13.

25. Burns, *Eadweard Muybridge*, pp. 18–22.

26. Ferrez and Naef, *Pioneer Photographers of Brazil*, p. 28.

27. Handlin, *Truth in History*, p. 241.

28. William R. Taylor, "Psyching Out the City," pp. 248–49.

29. Robert F. Berkhofer, Jr., *A Behavioral Approach to Historical Analysis*, pp. 133–34.

30. Shloss, *In Visible Light*, p. 267.

31. H. L. Hoffenberg, *Nineteenth-Century South American Photographs*, p. 107.

32. Handlin, *Truth in History*, p. 236, citing Fritz Saxl, "Veritas Filia Temporis," in Raymond Klibansky and H. J. Paton, eds., *Philosophy and History* (New York: Harper and Row, 1963), pp. 197ff; Erwin Panofsky, "Et in Arcadia Ego," in *Philosophy and History*, pp. 223ff.

33. Handlin, *Truth in History*, p. 237.

34. John W. Boddam-Whetham, *Across Central America*, p. 41, cited by Burns, *Eadweard Muybridge*, p. 71.

35. Like the film director Alfred Hitchcock, many of the early photographers included themselves in their compositions. Muybridge and Pannunzi did this regularly, for example. Courtesy of H. L. Hoffenberg.

36. Taylor, "Psyching Out the City," p. 250.

37. Beloff, *Camera Culture*. p. 157.

38. It is captioned "Los asesinos da Humaitá ejecutados el dia 6 de noviembre de 1874." See Boris Kossoy, *Origens e espansão da fotografia no Brasil: século XIX*.

39. See Edward Lucie-Smith, *The Invented Eye: Masterpieces of Photography, 1839–1914*, quoted by Beloff, *Camera Culture*, p. 67.

40. Courtesy of Steve Stein. Photograph from personal archive of Víctor Raul Haya de la Torre.

41. See Mejía, "Colombian Photographs," p. 52.

42. John Joseph Honigmann, *Culture and Personality* (New York: Harper & Row, 1954), p. 134, cited by John Collier, Jr., and Malcolm Collier, *Visual Anthropology: Photography as a Research Method*, p. 46.

43. See Julia Hirsch, *Family Photographs* (New York: Oxford University Press, 1981), pp. 12, 21, 51, 55.

44. Compare this photograph to 3.61 below, in terms of the levels in which the subjects are posed.

45. Gilbert M. Joseph, "Documenting a Regional Pastime: Baseball in Yucatán," in Robert M. Levine, ed., *Windows on Latin America*, p. 86.

46. See John Szarkowski, "Evening Lecture," in Eugenia Parry Janis and Wendy MacNeil, eds., *Photography Within the Humanities* (Danbury, New Hampshire: Addison House, 1977).

47. See Guilhermo Thorndike, *Autoretrato Peru: 1850–1900*, p. 99.

48. See Hoffenberg, *South America in Photographs*, pp. 141–42.

49. See Hoffenberg, *South America in Photographs*, p. 142.

50. The classic treatment of the armed struggle is by Euclydes da Cunha, *Os Sertões* (Rio de Janeiro, 1902).

51. See Robert M. Levine, "Mud-Hut Jerusalem: Canudos Revisited," *Hispanic American Historical Review* 68 (November 1988): 525–72.

52. See Boris Kossoy, "Os 30 Valérios," *History of Photography* 2 (January 1978): 22.

53. See, for example, Patricio Gross, Armando de Ramón, and Enrique Vial, *Imagen Ambiental de Santiago, 1880–1930*.

54. See Boris Kossoy, "Militão Augusto de Azevedo of Brazil: The Photographic Documentation of São Paulo (1862–1887)," p. 9.

55. Joel Snyder and Neil Walsh Allen, "Photography, Vision, and Representation"; Thomas F. Barrow, ed., *Reading into Photography* (Albuquerque: University of New Mexico Press, 1982), p. 62.

56. See Roland Barthes, *Camera Lucida: Reflections on Photography*, pp. 40–41.

57. See Collier and Collier, *Visual Anthropology*.

58. John Tagg, *The Burden of Representation. Essays on Photographies and Histories*, p. 187.

59. Keith McElroy, "Prisoner in Peru," p. 70. The photographer was Fernand Garreaud. Copies of the album may be found at the Peruvian National Library and in the Instituto Raul Porras Barrenechea in Lima.

4 Posed Worlds and Alternate Realities

1. Alan Trachtenberg, "The Camera and Dr. Barnardo," p. 71.

2. See Max Kozloff, "Opaque Disclosures," p. 151.

3. Michel Foucault, *Discipline and Punish: Birth of the Prison*, trans. A. Sheridan (London: Allen Lane, 1977), pp. 200–209, cited by John Tagg, *The Burden of Representation. Essays on Photographies and Histories*, pp. 85–86.

4. This photograph was discussed by Sandra Lauderdale Graham in her presentation, "Reading the Lives of the Poor" at the symposium "Nineteenth Century Brazilian Photography" at the University of New Mexico, Albuquerque, April 27, 1988.

5. Other *carte de visite* photographers posed Indian and black women with one or both breasts exposed. In most cases, there was no apparent compositional reason to do so: the motives must have been commercial. See the Maunouroy y Courret Hnos. *cartes* from the Archivo Prado in Lima reprinted in Guilhermo Thorndike, *Autoretrato: Peru 1850–1900*, p. 17.

6. H. L. Hoffenberg, *Nineteenth-Century South America in Photographs*, p. 27.

7. See Trachtenberg, "The Camera and Dr. Barnardo," 71.

8. Max Kozloff, "Chambi of Cuzco," pp. 107–108.

9. Courtesy of Fran Antmann.

10. Kozloff, "Opaque Disclosures," p. 145.

11. Kozloff, "Opaque Disclosures," p. 147.

12. See Harry B. Henderson, III, *Versions of the Past: The Historical Imagination in American Fiction*, pp. 8–9; Max Kozloff, "Report from the Region of Decayed Smiles," p. 23.

Glossary

Aguardente. Powerful alcoholic liquor made from sugar; crude rum.

Albumen. Photographic coating invented in the 1840s permitting the use of glass-plate negatives. It was superseded by the wet collodion process.

Ambrotype. A collodion positive printed on glass. See *Wet collodion*.

Amerindian. A native indigenous to the Americas.

APRA. A nationalist, Indianist political movement founded by Haya de la Torre and José Carlos Mariategui in Peru.

Brazilian Empire. Monarchical government headed by Emperors Pedro I and Pedro II, from 1822 to 1889.

Caboclo. An Indian who has adopted European ways; or a Brazilian of mixed European, Amerindian, and African origin.

Cacique. Amerindian chieftain or tribal leader.

Calotype. A negative/positive photographic process invented by Englishman William Henry Fox Talbot in 1841.

Camera lucida. An improved physiontrace, invented in 1807. See *Physiontrace*.

Camera obscura. A prephotographic device that transmits shadowy images to facilitate copying.

Campesinos. Indian peasants.

Canudos. Millenarian community in the Bahian backlands, crushed by Brazilian government forces in 1897.

Carioca. Resident of the city of Rio de Janeiro.

Carte de visite. A small, mass-produced photographic portrait affixed to a pasteboard, extremely popular in the 1850s.

Caudillo. Local strongman or boss, often a landowner or rancher. At the regional or national level, a political chief, sometimes employing methods of intimidation.

Choreometrics. The study of patterns of body behavior.

Civilista. Name given to the Brazilian presidential campaign of 1910–11; literally, "civilian," in contrast to the opposition candidate, the minister of war.

Costumbrista. Artist trained to reproduce scenes from nature in highly accurate detail.

Creole. Member of the colonial elite born in the New World and secondary in status to peninsulares. See *Peninsulares*.

Crown. In Spain, the Hapsburg dynasty followed by the Bourbons; in Portugal, the Bragança line.

Daguerreotype. Photographic image on a silvered copper plate usually of small dimensions. Named after its inventor, Louis-Jacques Mande Daguerre, who offered the patent to the world on August 19, 1839.

Dry-plate. Process using gelatin emulsions invented in 1871 by Englishman Richard Leach Maddox and which came into general use a decade later. The first Kodaks used a variant of the dry-plate system.

El Dorado. Legendary Amerindian city of vast riches and gold.

Ex voto. Carved figures, usually of wood, used in Afro-Brazilian healing rituals.

f 14. Small aperture lens opening permitting sharp detail but demanding a high amount of reflected light on the subject.

Favela. A Brazilian hillside slum common in Rio de Janeiro and São Paulo.

Fazendeiro (Port.); Hacendado (Span.). Owner of a rural property of medium or large size, sometimes a ranch, other times agricultural land.

Feira (Port.); Feria (Span.). A rural marketplace, usually held one day each week.

Gaucho. Cowboy of the Argentine, Uruguayan, and southern Brazilian pampas.

Gran Colombia. Former Spanish colonial viceroyalty encompassing present-day Colombia and Venezuela.

Guardia Civil. Militia, or civil guard.

Hacienda. A plantation, usually employing slave or Indian labor.

Henequén. A fibrous plant from which hemp is made, common in Mexico and Brazil.

Imperial. Referring to the Spanish and Portuguese overseas colonial empire. Cf. *Brazilian Empire*.

Indigenism. A movement advocating recognition of Indian rights and culture.

Kinesics. Study of body behavior and movement.

Laissez-faire. Literally, "hands-off." In political terms, a policy advocating minimal government control or intervention.

La Plata. Former Spanish colonial viceroyalty encompassing present-day Argentina, Uruguay, and Paraguay.

Lithograph. A print produced by a planographic (ink on stone) process, often based on a photograph.

Manto. Shawl.

Maté. An herbal tea common to southern South America, especially Paraguay, Argentina, and the Brazilian region of Mato Grosso.

Mestizo. Person of mixed Amerindian and European origin.

Mil Flores. Presidential palace, Caracas.

Milperos. Maize-growing peasants of the Yucatán, Mexico.

Mulatto. Person of mixed Negro and European origin.

Paulista. Resident of the city or state of São Paulo.

Peninsular. Referring to the Iberian peninsula nations of Spain and Portugal.

Peninsulares. Iberian-born men and women living in the New World. Their children, no matter how wealthy or powerful, received the secondary status of creoles. See *Creole*.

Photographic. French language term coined by French-Brazilian inventor Hercules Florence for his photographic process nearly a decade before Daguerre.

Physiontrace. Primitive device invented in 1786 to help artists copy facial outlines in portrait-making.

Positivism. A political and social philosophy advocating rule by an elite selected by talent and powers of reason.

Highly influential in nineteenth-century Argentina, Brazil, and Mexico.

Proxemics. Study of spatial relationships.

Republic (Brazil). National government inaugurated in 1889 after the fall of the monarchy.

Saya y manto. Peruvian costume worn by women of the elite consisting of a dark-colored shawl and skirt, draped in the Moorish manner.

Semiotics. The study of the meanings of signs and symbols.

Sertão. Backlands of rural Brazil, characterized by arid conditions and afflicted historically by periodic drought.

Stereographs. Photographs produced with a two-lensed camera and viewed on cards mounted on a binocular viewer, giving the impression of three-dimensionality.

War of the Pacific. Conflict between Peru and Chile, 1879–1883.

War of a Thousand Days. Civil war in Colombia, 1899–1902.

Wet collodion (or wet-plate). A photographic process invented in 1851 by Englishman Frederick Scott Archer, which reduced sharply the length of time needed to make a photographic image.

Yanaperos. Bolivian peasants squatting on patron's lands.

Yoruba culture. African cultural systems predominant in Cuba, Trinidad, and Brazil.

Zambo. Person of Afro-Amerindian origin.

Zapotec. Amerindian culture native to present-day Oaxaca, Mexico.

Sources of the Photographs

AM	Antonio Marcelino
BK	Boris Kossoy
BNC	Biblioteca Nacional, Caracas
BV	Bernardo Vega
CEEC	Centro de Estudos Euclydes da Cunha
CMP	California Museum of Photography
ES	Eduardo Serrano
EW	Elyn Welsh
FA	Frances Antmann
FN	Frederico Nasser
GF	Gilberto Ferrez
GJ	Gilbert M. Joseph
GMS	Gilda Mello e Souza
HH	H. L. Hoffenberg
IHB	Instituto Histórico da Bahia, Salvador
IJN	Instituto Joaquim Nabuco, Recife
IRPB	Instituto Raul Porras Barrenechea, Lima
JLS	José Luiz de Souza
LC	Library of Congress
LG	Lenny del Granado
MC	Manuel Chambi
MP	Moises Pitchón
RF	Ramiro Fernandez
SHSW	State Historical Society of Wisconsin
SS	Steve Stein
TU	Tulane University
UNM	University of New Mexico Zimmerman Library

Bibliography

Adorno, Theodor. *Negative Dialectics*. Translated by E. B. Ashton. New York: Seabury, 1973.

Aguiles, Nazor. *Caracas física y espiritual*. Caracas: Litografía Tecnocolor, 1977.

Album de Belém, Pará. 15 de novembro de 1902. Belém: F. A. Fidanza, 1902.

Album de Família: 1932. São Paulo: Livraria Martins Editôra, 1982.

Amaral, Aracy A.; Lemos, Carlos A. C.; and Bernardet, Jean-Claude. *Retratos quase inocentes*. São Paulo: Ed. Nobel, 1983.

Andrade, Mário de. *O turista aprendiz*. São Paulo: Duas Cidades, 1976.

Antmann, Frances. "La fotografía como elemento de analisis histórico-social." *Que Hacer?* 11 (1981):112–27.

———. "Sebastian Rodriguez's View from Within: The Work of an Andean Photographer in the Mining Town of Morococha, Peru, 1928 to 1968." Ph.D. dissertation, New York University, 1983.

Arendt, Hannah. Introduction to *Illuminations*, by Walter Benjamin. New York: Harcourt, Brace & World, 1968.

Assim Vivem os Italianos. Caxias do Sul, Brazil: Editora da Universidade de Caxias do Sul & Escola Superior de Teologia São Lourenço de Brindes, 1982.

Atkeret, Robert U. *Photoanalysis*. New York: Simon and Schuster, 1973.

Azevedo, Militão Augusto de. *Album Comparativo da Cidade de São Paulo, 1862–1887*. São Paulo, 1887.

Azevedo, Paulo Cesar, and Lissovsky, Mauricio. *Escravos Brasileiros do século xix na fotografía de Cristiano Jr.* São Paulo: Ex Libris, 1988.

Baker, Will. *Backwards: An Essay on Indians, Time and Photography*. Berkeley: North Atlantic Books, 1983.

Barnhard, Virginia, ed. *Elites, Masses, and Modernization in Latin America, 1850–1930*. Austin: University of Texas Press, 1979.

Barrow, Thomas, ed. *Reading into Photography*. Albuquerque: University of New Mexico Press, 1982.

Barthes, Roland. *Camera Lucida: Reflections on Photography*. Translated by Richard Howard. New York: Farrar, Straus & Giroux, 1981.

———. *Mythologies*. Translated by Annette Lavers. New York: Hill and Wang, 1972.

Barzun, Jacques, ed. *The Delights of Detection*. New York: Criterion Books, 1961.

Barzun, Jacques, and Graff, Henry F. *The Modern Researcher*. 4th ed. Orlando: Harcourt Brace Jovanovich, 1985.

Bayer, Jonathan. *Reading Photographs: Understanding the Aesthetics of Photography*. New York: Pantheon Books, 1977.

Becquer Casaballe, Amado, and Cuarterolo, Miguel Angel. *Cronica de la fotografía rioplatense, 1840–1940*. Buenos Aires: Editorial del Fotógrafo, 1983.

Beloff, Halla. *Camera Culture*. Oxford: Basil Blackwell Ltd., 1985.

Benjamin, Walter. *Illuminations*. New York: Harcourt, Brace & World, 1968.

———. "A Short History of Photography." Translated by Phil Patton. *Artforum* 15 (Feb. 1977):46–51.

Berger, John. *About Looking*. New York: Pantheon Books, 1980.

Berger, John, and Mohr, Jean. *Another Way of Telling*. New York: Pantheon Books, 1982.

Berger, Paulo. *O Rio de ontem no cartão postal, 1900–1930*. Rio de Janeiro: Prefeitura da Cidade do Rio de Janeiro, 1983.

Berkhofer, Robert F., Jr. *A Behavorial Approach to Historical Analysis*. New York: The Free Press, 1969.

Bernard, Gaëlle, ed. *L'Enfant et la Photographie*. Paris: Centre Georges Pompidou, 1982.

Billeter, Erika. "Bilder einer Ausstellung." *Fotografie Lateinamerika von 1860 bis heute*. Bern, Switzerland: Künsthaus Zurich/Beneli Verlag, 1981.

Birdwhistell, Ray L. *Kinesics and Context*. Philadelphia: University of Pennsylvania Press, 1970.

Blackman, Margaret B. Introduction to *From Site to Sight: Anthropology, Photography, and the Power of Imagery* by Melissa Banta and Curtis M. Hinsley. Cambridge: Peabody Museum Press, 1986.

Bloch, Marc. *The Historian's Craft*. Translated by Peter Putnam. New York: Vintage Books, 1953.

Bloom, Lisa. "Charles De Forest Fredricks: 19th Century

Entrepreneur in the Photography Industry." Master's thesis, Visual Studies Workshop, New York, Spring 1983.

Boddam-Whetham, John W. *Across Central America*. London: Hurst & Blackett, 1877.

Braive, Michel F. *The Photograph: A Social History*. Translated by David Britt. New York: McGraw-Hill, 1966.

Brenner, Anita. *The Wind that Swept Mexico: The History of the Mexican Revolution, 1910–1942*. New York, 1943.

Brown, Bryan, ed. *The England of Henry Taunt, Victorian Photographer*. London: Routledge & Kegan Paul, c. 1970.

Buckland, Gail. *Reality Recorded: Early Documentary Photography*. Greenwich, Connecticut: New York Graphic Society, 1974.

Burgin, Victor. *Thinking Photography*. London: Macmillan, 1982.

Burns, E. Bradford. *Eadweard Muybridge in Guatemala, 1875: The Photographer as Social Recorder*. Berkeley: University of California Press, 1987.

———. *Nationalism in Brazil*. New York: Praeger Publishers, 1968.

Burston, W. H., and Green, C. W., eds. *Handbook for History Teachers*. London: Methuen Educational, 1962.

Canales, Claudia. *Romualdo García, un fotógrafo, una ciudad, una época*. Guanajato, Mexico: Gobierno del Estado, 1980.

Carril, Bonifácio del, and Aguirre Saravia, Aníbal G. *Iconografía de Buenos Aires: la ciudad de Garay hasta 1852*.

Buenos Aires: Municipalidad de la Ciudad de Buenos Aires, 1982.

Casasola, Gustavo. *História gráfica de la Revolución Mexicana, 1900–1960. Edición Commemorativa*. Mexico City: Ed. F. Trillas, 1964.

Catlin, S. L., and Grieder, T. *Art of Latin America since Independence*. New Haven: Yale University Press, 1966.

Chevedden, Paul. "Making Light of Everything: Early Photography of the Middle East and Current Photomania." *Middle Eastern Studies Association Bulletin* 18 (December 1984): 151–74.

Clark, G. Kitson. *Guide for Research Students Working on Historical Subjects*. London: Cambridge University Press, 1938.

Cockcroft, Eva. "Art and Politics in Latin America." *Art in America* 69 (October 1981): 37–40.

Coke, Van Deren. *The Painter and the Photographer*. Albuquerque: University of New Mexico Press, 1972.

Coleman, A. D. "Crossed Borders, Common Ground." *The Mining Town of Morococha*. Exhibit Catalog, Museum of Contemporary Hispanic Art, New York, 1987.

———. *Light Readings: A Photography Critic's Writings, 1968–1978*. New York: Oxford University Press, 1979.

Collier, John, Jr., and Collier, Malcolm. *Visual Anthropology: Photography as a Research Method*. Rev. ed. Albuquerque: University of New Mexico Press, 1986.

Collins, Kathleen. "Portraits of Slave Children." *History of Photography* 9: 187–208.

Conger, Amy. *Edward Weston in Mexico, 1923–1926*. San Francisco: San Francisco Museum of Modern Art, 1983.

———. "Reflections on Latin American Photography." *Afterimage*, March 1985, pp. 4–5.

Costa, Helouise, and Rodrigues, Renato. "O reverso da modernidade." *Folhetim (Folha de S. Paulo)*, no. 559, October 23, 1987, pp. B-10–11.

Crawford, William. *The Keepers of Light: A History and Working Guide to Early Photographic Processes*. Dobbs Ferry, New York: Morgan & Morgan, 1979.

Croce, Benedetto. *History: Its Theory and Practice*. Translated by Douglas Ainslie. New York: Harcourt, Brace and Company, 1921.

Cuenca, Humberto. *Imagen literaria del periodismo*. Mexico City: Ed. Cultural Venezolano, 1961.

Davidson, James West and Lytle, Mark Hamilton. *After the Fact: the Art of Historical Detection*. 2nd ed. New York: Alfred A. Knopf, 1986.

Davis, Thomas L. *Shoots: A Guide to Your Family's Photographic Heritage*. Danbury, New Hampshire: Addison House, 1978.

Day, Holliday T. "Fotografia Polska, 1838–1979." *Art in America* 68 (January 1980): 37–39.

Dorronsoro, Josune. *Significación histórica de la fotografía*. Caracas: Equinoccio, 1981.

Doctorow, E. L. "False Documents." *American Review* 26 (December 1977).

Eakle, Arlene H. *Photographic Analysis*. Bountiful, Utah: Faisal, 1976.

Earle, Edward W. "Why Photography? Its Place in Our Culture." *California Museum of Photography Bulletin* 4 (1984): 43–48.

Eco, Umberto. *A Theory of Semiotics*. Bloomington: Indiana University Press, 1976.

Ellul, Jacques. *Propaganda, the Formation of Men's Attitudes*. New York: Vintage Books, 1973.

English, Donald E. *The Political Uses of Photography in the Third French Republic, 1871–1914*. Ann Arbor: University of Michigan Research Press, 1984.

Escobar, Felipe, ed. *Melitón Rodríguez, fotografías*. Bogotá: Ed. Ancora Editores, 1985.

Fabian, Ranier, and Adam, H. Christian. *Frühe Reisen mit der Kamera*. Hamburg: Stern, 1981.

Fagg, John Edwin. *Latin America: A General History*. New York: Macmillan, 1963.

Fernandez, José Maria Saldana. "La Fotografía en el Rio de la Plata." *La Prensa* (Buenos Aires), January 26, 1938.

Fernandez, Ramiro. "Cuba: Fotografia 1860–1920, Selected Images from the Collection of Ramiro Fernandez." In *Windows on Latin America: Understanding Society Through Photographs*, edited by Robert M. Levine. Coral Gables: SECOLAS, 1987, pp. 9–32.

Ferrez, Gilberto. *A fotografia no Brasil, 1840–1900*. Rio de Janeiro: FUNARTE, 1985.

Ferrez, Gilberto and Naef, Weston J. *Pioneer Photographers of Brazil: 1840–1920*. New York: Center for Inter-American Relations, 1976.

Ferro, Marc. *Analyse de films, analyse de sociétés*. Paris: Hachette, 1975.

———. *The Use and Abuse of History, or, How the Past Is Taught*. London: Routledge & Kegan Paul, 1984.

Flynn, Peter. *Brazil: A Political Analysis*. Boulder: Westview Press, 1978.

Fondiller, Harvey V. Review of *The World of Agustín Víctor Casasola: Mexico, 1900–1938*, exhibit at the International Center for Photography, New York, Feb. 22–March 24, 1985. *Popular Photography*, May 1985, p. 74.

Fontanella, Lee. *La historia de la fotografía en España desde sus origens hasta 1900*. Madrid: El Viso, 1981.

Forgus, R. H. *Perception*. New York: McGraw-Hill, 1970. Fox Talbot, W. H. *The Pencil of Nature*. London, 1844.

Freund, Gisèle. *La Photographie en France au dixneuvième siècle*. Paris, 1936.

———. *Photography and Society*. Boston: David R. Godine, 1980.

Freyre, Gilberto. *O escravo nos anúncios de jornais brasileiros do século XIX*. Recife: Fundação Joaquim Nabuco, 1963.

———. *Mansions and the Shanties*. Translated by Harriet de Onis. New York: Alfred A. Knopf, 1963.

———. *Retratos de jornais velhos*. 2nd ed. Rio de Janeiro: MEC, 1964.

———. *Sociologia*. 2nd ed. Rio de Janeiro: José Olympio Editora, 1957.

———. *Vida social no Brasil nos meados do século XIX*. Recife: Fundação Joaquim Nabuco, 1964.

Freyre, Gilberto, editor. *O Retrato brasileiro. Fotografias da Coleção Francisco Rodrigues, 1840–1920*. Rio de Janeiro: FUNARTE/ MEC, 1983.

Frond, Victor. *Album de vistas, panoramas, monumentos, costumes*. Paris, 1861.

Galassi, Peter. *Before Photography: Painting and the Invention of Photography*. New York: Museum of Modern Art, 1981.

Gaudin, Marc Antoine. *Traité pratique de photographie*. Paris: J. J. Dubochet, 1844.

Gernsheim, Helmut. *The Origins of Photography*. New York: Thames and Hudson, 1982.

Goode, William J. *The Celebration of Heroes: Prestige as a Social Control System*. Berkeley: University of California Press, 1978.

Gordon, Colin. *A Richer Dust: Echoes from an Eduardian Album*. New York: Lippincott, 1978.

Governo do Estado de São Paulo. *Memória Paulistano*. São Paulo: Secretária de Cultura, Esportes e Turismo, 1975.

Graham-Brown, Sarah. *Images of Women. The Portrayal of Women in Photography of the Middle East, 1860–1950*. London: Quartet Books Ltd., 1988.

Gross, Patricio; de Ramón, Armando; and Vial, Enrique. *Imagen ambiental de Santiago: 1880–1930*. 2nd ed. Santiago: Ediciones Universidad Católica de Chile, 1985.

Gutman, Judith Mara. *Through Indian Eyes: 19th and 20th Century Photography from India*. New York: Oxford University Press, International Center of Photography, 1982.

Haas, Robert Bartlett. *Muybridge, Man in Motion*. Berkeley: University of California Press, 1976.

Haberly, David T. *Three Sad Races: Racial Identity and National Consciousness in Brazilian Literature*. Cambridge: Cambridge University Press, 1983.

Hales, Peter Bacon. *Silver Cities: The Photography of American Urbanization, 1839–1915*. Philadelphia: Temple University Press, 1984.

————. *William Henry Jackson and the Transformation of the American Landscape*. Philadelphia: Temple University Press, 1988.

Hall, Edward T. *The Hidden Dimension*. New York: Doubleday, 1966.

————. *The Silent Language*. New York: Doubleday, 1959.

Handlin, Oscar. *Truth in History*. Cambridge, Massachusetts: Harvard University Press, 1979.

Harris, Marvin. *Town and Country in Brazil: A Socio-Anthropological Study of a Small Brazilian Town*. New York: Norton, 1956.

Henderson, Harry B., III. *Versions of the Past: The Historical Imagination in American Fiction*. New York: Oxford University Press, 1974.

Heyert, Elizabeth. *The Glass House Years: Victorian Portrait Photography, 1839–1870*. Montclair, England and London: Allanheld & Schram/ George Prior, 1979.

Hiley, Michael. *Seeing Through Photographs*. London: Gordon Fraser, 1983.

Hinchliff, Thomas Woodbine. *South American Sketches*. London: Longman, Roberts & Green, 1863.

Hirsch, Julia. *Family Portraits: Content, Meaning, and Effect*. New York: Oxford University Press, 1981.

Hoffenberg, H. L. *Nineteenth-Century South America in Photographs*. New York: Dover Publications, 1982.

Holt, Glen E. "Chicago Through a Camera Lens: An Essay on Photography as History." *Chicago History* 1 (Spring 1971): 158–75.

im Thurn, E. F. "Anthropological Uses of the Camera." *The Journal of the Anthropological Institute of Great Britain and Ireland* 23 (1893).

Instituto Autonomo Biblioteca Nacional y de Servicios de Bibliotecas. *Origenes de la fotografía en Venezuela*. Caracas: IABNSB, 1978.

International Center of Photography. *ICP Encyclopedia of Photography*. New York: Photographic Book Company, 1979.

Izquierdo, Julio Philippi, ed. *Vistas de Chile por Rudolfo Amando Philippi*. Santiago: Editorial Universitaria, 1973.

Jammes, Marie-Thérèse, and Jammes, André. "Egypt in Flaubert's Time: The First Photographers, 1839–1860." *Aperture*, no. 78 (1977), pp. 62–64.

Janis, Eugenia Parry, and MacNeil, Wendy, eds. *Photography Within the Humanities*. Danbury, New Hampshire: Addison House, 1977.

Jeffrey, Ian. *Photography: A Concise History*. New York: Oxford University Press, 1981.

Jones, Colonel J. Bascom, ed. *El "Libro Azul" de Guatemala/The "Blue Book" of Guatemala, 1915*. New Orleans: Searcy & Pfaff, 1915.

Jussim, Estelle. *Visual Communication and the Graphic Arts: Photographic Technologies in the Nineteenth Century*. Boston: Bowker, 1978.

Karmel, Pepe. "Terra Incognita." *Art in America* 71 (October 1983):37–43.

Kennedy, John M. *A Psychology of Picture Perception*. San Francisco: Jossey-Bass, 1974.

Klett, Mark. "Subject, Vantage Point, Viewpoint: Factors in Rephotography." *Exposure*, Fall 1979, pp. 49-55.

Kossoy, Boris. *Hercules Florence. 1833: A descoberta isolada de fotografía no Brasil*. São Paulo: Livraria Duas Cidades, 1976.

————. "Marc Ferrez." In *ICP Encyclopedia of Photography*. New York: Photographic Book Company, 1979.

————. "Antoine Hercules Florence." In *ICP Encyclopedia of Photography*. New York: Photographic Book Company, 1979.

————. "Militão Augusto de Azevedo of Brazil: The Photographic Documentation of São Paulo (1862–1887)." *History of Photography* 4 (January 1980):9–17.

————. *Origens e expansão da fotografia no Brasil: Século xix*, Rio de Janeiro: MEC/FUNARTE, 1978.

Koster, Henry. *Travels in Brazil*. 2 vols. London: Longman, Hurst, Rees, Orme & Brown, 1817.

Kouwenhoven, John A. "The Snapshot." *Aperture* 19 (1974).

Kozloff, Max. "Chambi of Cuzco." *Art in America* 67 (December 1979):107–11.

———. "Opaque Disclosures." *Art in America* 75 (October 1987):144–153.

———. *Photography & Fascination*. Essays. Danbury, New Hampshire: Addison House, 1979.

———. *The Privileged Eye: Essays on Photography*. Albuquerque: University of New Mexico Press, 1987.

———. "Report from the Region of Decayed Smiles." *Art in America* 68 (April 1980):23–39.

Krims, Leslie. *Fictocryptokrimsographs*. New York: Humpy Press, 1975.

Larrea, D. F. Eguren de. *El Cusco, su vida, sus maravillas*. Lima: Vias de Comunicación Del Peru (Empresa Excelsior), 1929.

Lesy, Michael. "The Photography of History." *Afterimage*, February 1975, pp. 2–3.

———. "Snapshots: Psychological Documents" *Afterimage*, October 1976, pp. 12–13.

———. *Wisconsin Death Trip*. New York: Pantheon, 1973.

Levene, Gustavo Gabriel, ed. *Historia ilustrada de la Argentina desde la colonia hasta nuestros días*. Buenos Aires: C. G. Fabril Editora, n.d.

Levine, Robert M., ed. *Windows on Latin America: Understanding Society Through Photographs*. Coral Gables: SECOLAS, 1987.

Licht, Fred. "Class Acts." *Art in America* 72 (January 1984):40–42.

Liébert, A. *La Photographie en Amérique*. 20th ed. Paris: A. Liébert, 1874.

Loke, Margaret. "Frozen in Time." *New York Times Magazine*, October 4, 1987, pp. 47–49.

Lopez, Barry. *Arctic Dreams: Imagination and Desire in a Northern Landscape*. Toronto and New York: Bantam Books, 1986.

Lucie-Smith, Edward. *The Invented Eye: Masterpieces of Photography, 1839–1914*. London: Paddington Press, 1975.

Luebke, Frederick C. *Germans in Brazil: A Comparative History of Cultural Conflict during World War I*. Baton Rouge: Louisiana State University Press, 1987.

Maas, Jeremy. *The Victorian Art World in Photographs*. New York: Universe Books, 1984.

McAlister, Lyle M. *Spain and Portugal in the New World, 1492–1700*. Minneapolis: University of Minnesota Press, 1984.

McCauley, Elizabeth Anne. *A. A. E. Disdéri and the Carte de Visite Photograph*. New Haven: Yale University Press, 1985.

McElroy, Keith. "The Daguerrean Era in Peru, 1839–1859." *History of Photography* 3 (April 1979):111–22.

———. *Early Peruvian Photography: A Critical Case Study*. Ann Arbor: University of Michigan Research Press, 1985.

———. "Montage or Reportage?" *History of Photography* 3 (July 1979):232.

———. "Photography in Depth." *History of Photography* 3 (April 1979):132.

———. "Prisoner in Peru." *History of Photography* 3 (January 1979):70.

———. "La Tapada Limeña: The Iconography of the Veiled Woman in 19th-Century Peru." *History of Photography* 5 (April 1981):133–47.

McNeill, William H. *Mythistory and Other Essays*. Chicago: University of Chicago Press, 1986.

Malcolm, Janet. *Diana and Nikon: Essays on the Aesthetics of Photography*. Boston: David Godine, 1980.

Mar, Timothy T. *Face Reading*. New York: Signet Books, 1974.

Margolis, Eric. "Mining Photographs: Unearthing the Meaning of Historical Photos." *Radical History Review* 40 (1985):133–49.

Martim, Ricardo [Guilherme Auler]. "Dom Pedro e a fotografia," Part I. *Tribuna de Petrópolis*, April 1, 1956.

Martín Chambi: Fotografía del Perú, 1920–1950. Buenos Aires: La Azotea Editorial Fotográfica, 1985.

Mejía, Germán Rodrigo. "Colombian Photographs of the Nineteenth and Early Twentieth Centuries." In *Windows* on *Latin America*, edited by Robert M. Levine. Coral Gables: SECOLAS, 1987, pp. 49–62.

Mello e Souza, Gilda de. *O espírito das roupas: a moda no século dezenove*. São Paulo: Companhia das Letras, 1987.

Moch, Leslie Page, and Stark, Gary D., eds. *Essays on the Family and Historical Change*. College Park: Texas A & M University Press, 1983.

Morse, Richard M. "Claims of Political Tradition." In *Readings in Latin American History*, edited by Peter J. Bakewell, John J. Johnson, and Meredith D. Dodge. Durham, North Carolina: Duke University Press, 1985.

Moutoussamy-Ashe, Jeanne. *Viewfinders: Black Women Photographers*. New York: Dodd, Mead & Co., 1986.

Mraz, John. "Particularidad y nostalgia." *Nexos* (Mexico City), July 1985, pp. 9–12.

Nabuco, Joaquim. *O Abolicionismo*. Translated and edited by Robert Conrad. Urbana: University of Illinois Press, 1977.

Naef, Weston. "Hercules Florence, 'Inventor do Photografia'." *Artforum*, February 1976.

Nesbit, Molly. "The Use of History." *Art in America* 72 (February 1986):72–83.

Newhall, Beaumont. *The Daguerreotype in America*. 3rd ed. New York: Dover Publications, 1976.

———. *The History of Photography from 1839 to Present*. New York: Museum of Modern Art, 1982.

"New World Africans: Nineteenth Century Images of Blacks in South America and the Caribbean." Catalog of the Schomburg Center for Research in Black Culture exhibition, May 2–September 7, 1985, New York.

Neyra, Hugo. "Tiempos de Courret: la vida y las ideas del 900." *Fanal* (Lima), August 1963, pp. 13–28.

Nochlin, Linda. *Realism*. New York: Penguin Books, 1977.

Panunzi, Benito. *Vistas y costumbres de Buenos Aires*. Buenos Aires, 1865.

Pereira, Eugenio S. "El centenario de la fotografía en Chile, 1840–1940." *Boletin de la Academia Chilena de la Historia*, no. 20 (1942).

Perl, Jed. "Japan: Photographs 1854–1905." *Art in America* 68 (February 1980):35–37.

Preiswerk, Roy, and Perrot, Dominique. *Ethnocentrisme et histoire*. Paris: Anthropos, 1975.

Pressacco, Alfredo Santos. "Hercules Florence, primeiro fotógrafo de América?" *Fotocamera* (Rio de Janeiro), no. 172, December 1965, pp. 61–62.

Pyle, David. "The Ethnographic Photography of W. D. Smithers." In *Perspectives on Photography*, edited by D. Oliphant and T. Zigal. Austin: Humanities Research Center, 1982.

Ramer, Richard C. "Daguerreotypes." *Catalog*. New York: R. C. Ramer, 1987, p. 32.

"Reciprocal Influence." *Princeton Alumni Weekly*, October 23, 1985, p. 16.

Ridings, Eugene W. "Foreign Predominance among Overseas Traders in Nineteenth-Century Latin America." *Latin American Research Review* 20 (1985):3–28.

Riobo, Júlio Felipe. *Daguerrotipos y retratos sobre vidrio en Buenos Aires, 1843–1873*. Buenos Aires, 1942.

Root, Marcus A. *The Camera and the Pencil, or the Heliographic Art*. 1864. Reprint. Philadelphia: Helios, 1970.

Rudisill, Richard. *Mirror Image: The Influence of the Daguerreotype on American Society*. Albuquerque: University of New Mexico Press, 1971.

Rugendas, João Maurício. *Viagem pitoresca através do Brasil*. Translated by Sérgio Milliet. 5th ed. São Paulo: Livraria Martins Editôra, 1941.

Rundell, Walter Jr. "Photographs as Historical Evidence: Early Texas Oil." *The American Archivist* 41 (October 1978).

Rybczynski, Witold. *Home: A Short History of an Idea*. New York: Viking, 1986.

Samanez, Hugo Neira. "Tiempos de Courret: La vida y las ideas del 900." *Clima* (Lima), August 1963, pp. 13–28.

Samuel, Raphael, ed. *People's History and Socialist Theory*. London: Routledge & Kegan Paul, 1981.

São Paulo: onde está sua história. São Paulo: Museu de Arte de São Paulo Assis Chateaubriand, 1981.

Scharf, Aaron. *Art and Photography*. 2nd ed. Baltimore: Penguin Books, 1975.

Schiller, Dan. "Realism, Photography, and Journalistic

Objectivity in 19th Century America." *Studies in the Anthropology of Visual Communication, vol. 4.* Philadelphia: Annenberg School of Communications, 1977.

Schwartz, Heinrich. *David Octavius Hill.* New York: Viking Press. 1931.

Scott, Rebecca. *Slave Emancipation in Cuba: The Transition to Free Labor, 1860–1899.* Princeton: Princeton University Press, 1985.

Serrano, Eduardo. *Historia de la fotografía en Colombia.* Bogotá: Museu de Arte Moderno, 1983.

Shloss, Carol. *In Visible Light. Photography and the American Writer: 1840–1940.* New York: Oxford University Press, 1987.

Silberman, Robert. "Our Town." *Art in America* 73 (July 1985):100–107.

Singleton, Charles S., ed. *Interpretation: Theory and Practice.* Baltimore: Johns Hopkins University Press, 1969.

Skidmore, Thomas E., and Smith, Peter H. *Modern Latin America.* New York and Oxford: Oxford University Press, 1984.

Snyder, Joel, and Allen, Neil Walsh. "Photography, Vision, and Representation." *Afterimage,* January 1976, pp. 8–13.

Sobieszek, Robert. "Historical Commentary." *Aperture* 15 (Spring 1970):iv–xi.

———. Introduction to "Hercules Florence, Pioneer of Photography in Brazil," by Boris Kossoy. *Image* 10 (March 1977).

Solomon-Godeau, Abigail. *Print Collector's Newsletter* 12 (January–February 1982):173–75.

Sontag, Susan. *On Photography.* New York: Farrar, Strauss and Giroux, 1977.

Stasz, Clarice. "The Early History of Visual Sociology." In *Images of Information: Still Photography in the Social Science,* edited by Jon Wagner. Beverly Hills: Sage Publications, 1979.

Steel, D. J., and Taylor, L. *Family History in Schools.* London: Phillimore and Co., 1973.

Stepan, Nancy. *Beginnings of Brazilian Science.* New York: Science History Publications, 1976.

Susman, Warren I. *Culture as History: The Transformation of American Society in the Twentieth Century.* New York: Pantheon Books, 1984.

Szarkowski, John. *American Photography Since 1960.* Boston: New York Graphic Society, 1978.

Tagg, John. *The Burden of Representation. Essays on Photographies and Histories.* Amherst: University of Massachusetts Press, 1988.

Talbot, George. *At Home: Domestic Life in the Post-Centennial Era, 1876–1920.* Madison: The State of Wisconsin Historical Society, 1976.

Taylor, William R. "Psyching Out the City." In *Uprooted Americans: Essays to Honor Oscar Handlin,* edited by Richard L. Bushman, Neil Harris, David Rothman, Barbara Miller Solomon, Stephan Thernstrom. Boston & Toronto: Little, Brown & Co., 1979.

Thomas, Alan. *Time in a Frame: Photography and the Nineteenth-Century Mind.* New York: Schocken Books, 1977.

Thorndike, Guillermo. *Autoretrato Peru: 1850–1900.* Lima: Editorial Universo, 1979.

Todd, Louise. "Richard Avedon's Imagined West." *Atlantic,* March 1986, pp. 101–3.

Trachtenberg, Alan. "The Camera and Dr. Barnardo." *Aperture* 19 (1975):68–77.

Vanderwood, Paul J. "Agustín Casasola in Context." *Proceedings of the Pacific Coast Council on Latin American Studies* 8 (1981–82):127–31.

Varnedoe, Kirk. "The Artifice of Candor: Impressionism and Photography Reconsidered." *Art in America* 68 (January 1980):66–78.

Vasquez, Pedro. *Dom Pedro II e a Fotografia no Brasil.* Rio de Janeiro: Fundação Roberto Marinho, 1985.

———. "Brazilian Photography in the Nineteenth Century." Exhibition Catalog to show at Maxwell Museum, University of New Mexico, April/May 1988.

———. *Fotografia: Reflexos e Reflexões.* Porto Alegre: L & PM Editores, 1986.

Vega, Bernardo. *Imágenes del Ayer.* Santo Domingo: Fundación Cultural Dominicana, 1980.

Veyne, Paul. *Comment on écrit l'histoire.* Paris: Le Seuil, 1971.

Vidal, Hernán García. *História ilustrada de la Guerra del Pacífico.* Santiago: Editorial Universitaria, 1979.

Vincent, Frank. *Around and About South America: Twenty Months of Quest and Query*. New York: D. Appleton & Company, 1903.

Viotti da Costa, Emília. *The Brazilian Empire: Myths and Realities*. Chicago: University of Chicago Press, 1985.

Wagner, Jon, ed. *Images of Information: Still Photography in the Social Sciences*. Beverly Hills: Sage Publications, 1979.

Walch, Peter, and Barrow, Thomas F., eds. *Perspectives on Photography: Essays in Honor of Beaumont Newhall*. Albuquerque: University of New Mexico Press, 1986.

Weber, Eugen. *Peasants into Frenchmen: The Modernization of Rural France, 1870–1914*. Stanford: Stanford University Press, 1976.

Welling, William, *Photography in America. The Formative Years, 1839–1900*. 1978. Reprint Albuquerque: University of New Mexico Press, 1988.

Wolf, Daniel, ed. *The American Space: Meaning in Nineteenth-Century Landscape Photography*. Middletown, Connecticut: Wesleyan University Press, 1985.

Zakia, Richard D. *Perception and Photography*. Englewood Cliffs, N.J.: Prentice-Hall, 1975.

Zaluar, A. E. *Peregrinação pela provincia de São Paulo (1860–61)*. São Paulo: Cultura, 1943.

Zuñige, Solange; Guilherme, Luíz; and Silva, Eduardo. *História Visual: Rio de Janeiro: condições de vida na la República*. Rio de Janeiro: FCRB-CNRC, 1986.

Index

About the Author

Robert M. Levine is Professor and Chairman of History at the University of Miami. He has published two monographs about Brazil and eight other books on Latin American subjects. His videotaped documentary "Imagenes de Reinos," which was produced in English, Spanish, Portuguese, and Chinese, won the 1986 Award of Merit of the Latin American Studies Association. He is past chairman of the Columbia University Seminars on Latin America and Brazil and of the national Committee on Brazilian Studies of the Conference of Latin American history.